Dianne Wilkinson

THE LIFE AND TIMES OF A GOSPEL SONGWRITER

DIANNE WILKINSON
with Daniel J. Mount

Copyright © 2012 Dianne Wilkinson and Daniel J. Mount

Published in Arden, North Carolina by Daniel J. Mount of
www.southerngospelblog.com.

Visit Dianne Wilkinson online at www.diannewilkinson.com.

Cover image courtesy of James Strayhorn Photography.

Cover design courtesy of Taylor Garms, Lacheln Designs.

ISBN: 0615680739
ISBN-13: 978-0615680736

CONTENTS

Introduction

It was fitting that the process of writing this unforgettable storyteller's autobiography began with an unforgettable story.

I had arranged to interview Dianne Wilkinson at the 2009 National Quartet Convention for my Southern Gospel news website, www.southerngospelblog.com. We began the interview about thirty minutes before the evening's program ended. She began telling many of the stories you're about to read; before I realized it, over an hour had passed.

Surely, I thought, people would still be wrapping things up after the night's events. I was wrong; the building was practically empty.

Dianne, her friend Gail Davison, and I walked out to our cars and drove out to the main exit gate.

It was locked.

We decided to drive around back and check the back exit.

It was also locked.

It looked like we had gotten locked in for the night! But finally, we found a little side exit with a security checkpoint. A guard wrote our names on his notepad and let us out.

Ever since that memorable day, I knew her story needed to become a book.

It took me over a year to work up the courage to suggest that she write an autobiography. When I brought up the idea in May 2011, she said that songwriting kept her so busy that she might never find the time. (She writes, on average, more than one song per week, and over two-thirds of those songs get recorded!)

So I offered to do a series of interviews and turn them into a book. She agreed, and this is the result.

Acknowledgments

Whenever a person is allowed to do a wonderful thing for a very long time and have any measure of success and joy along the way, there are many people who have contributed and helped to make it possible. I'd like to mention some of these, with my heartfelt thanks.

I want to thank the artists who have recorded my songs from 1976 up to the present day. The songs would not help anyone if they were all still resting in stacks in my piano stool. You have sung the messages in the songs all over the country and beyond and brought life to the songs beyond what I might have imagined. And with *so* many of you, I have some of the sweetest and dearest friendships of any in my life.

I owe a great debt to the publishing people who have worked so hard for me—first, Niles Borop at Centergy Music in the early 2000s, and Rick Shelton and the other good folks at Daywind from 2005 forward. It has been a joy to work with all of you, and all of you have been wonderful to me.

I'd like to thank everyone involved in radio—the people at the record companies who send the songs out and stay in touch with the deejay, the folks who decide what to include on the play lists and "spin the platters"—*all* of you. People hear my songs on the radio who would never go to church, so you are a vital part of my writing ministry.

I want to thank my fellow Gospel songwriters, who are like family to me, who encourage me and inspire me in ways they don't even know. I love all of you!

I owe a huge debt of thanks to Terry Franklin, Tim Parton, Matthew Holt, Adam Kohout, and other great singers and musicians who have done my demos over the years. I know how hard you work, and I know the high standards you have. All of you are amazing talents, and your contribution to my writing ministry is immeasurable.

I want to thank all the people involved in getting the songs recorded—the producer/arrangers, the musicians, background vocalists, engineers, the people who do the mixing—anyone and everyone who moves the song from the demo onto a CD or some other medium, fully fleshed out and orchestrated—and so often sounding like what I heard in my head when I wrote it, only so much more. You are the folks we don't see—serving in the background, using your amazing gifts for the glory of God.

I want to remember some people who have already gone Home and who had much to do with Dianne Wilkinson becoming a songwriter and *still* being blessed to write today. My dear Grandmother; my Mama, Blanche Branscum; my Aunt Mavis

Harris; Joe Kelsey, who first walked up to me and said, "Dianne, we want to record your song"; my late husband, Tim, who was such an encourager to me and was always my biggest fan; and Glen and George and Roger of the Cathedral Quartet, along with the other dear men who sang with them through the years. They are probably the reason people know my name today.

I want to thank the fans of Southern Gospel music who contact me often and tell me that the songs have been a blessing to them and that they are praying for me. They are the fans of the best music in the world!

I want to thank my dear family and my personal friends, inside and outside the music business, who have encouraged me through the years. So many of them inspire me with their Christian testimony. I include my church family in this group, both now at Springhill and at all the other churches where I have been—God bless all of you!

I want to thank Daniel Mount, who had the idea for this book, and who worked tirelessly over a long period of time interviewing me and doing everything that has to be done to produce a book. He is a young man who has become a very dear friend, and he is also Godly and wise beyond his years. No one ever had a better friend!

I saved the Best for last. I thank my Heavenly Father for charting my course in His Divine foreknowledge before I was ever born and for moving me through life and connecting me with the right people and putting me in the right places to see that His plan was carried out. I thank Him for calling me into His Word when I was very young and causing me to love it so—even when I didn't know what His plan was. I thank Him for the music, which has been all joy to me from the time I fell in love with it when I was a little girl. Most of all, I thank Him for sending his Dear Son to die for my sins, and for saving my soul in 1974, and for the abundant life He has given me *all* the way through. Praise His Wonderful Name!!

- Dianne Wilkinson

Thank you to Gail Davison, Brian Crout, Hannah Grady, Mason Mount, Mary Mount, Deborah Mount, Bethany Mount, Michael Mount, Ruthanne Mount, Gabriel Mount, David Garms, Kris Garms, Benjamin Garms, Taylor Garms, Leesha Garms, Samuel Garms, Jayme Garms, and Caleb Garms for reading the draft and making many helpful suggestions and corrections.

Thank you to Taylor Garms for the front and back cover graphic design.

Thank you to Miss Dianne for entrusting me with this story. Also, thank you for letting me keep your idiomatic Southern expressions in the text—I *love* the way you talk!

Thank you to God for saving us and for giving Miss Dianne so many songs for us to sing.

- Daniel J. Mount

1

When God has a plan for your life, He starts early on making that happen. But when He has a plan for your life, He has claims on your life. If you ever lose your awareness of His claims on your life, He won't get the best of what you have to offer.

My beginnings weren't great. Some people would say I started out behind the eight ball. But somehow, always, I had the whispering from the Lord, "Your end will be better than your beginning." That has been so true in my life.

John Allen Turner Hardin, my great-granddaddy, left us a rich heritage. He fought in the Civil War and was a state representative in Mississippi. In those days, the Hardins were Mississippi people. He had land in a little farming community called Potts Camp, located in Marshall County. His wife's name was Isabella, and they had eleven children. (Of course, back then, everyone had big families!)

Not long after World War I, people in that whole little part of Marshall County began to hear about the rich farmland in northeast Arkansas, up in the Mississippi Delta. They sent some people over to scout it out. A whole settlement of those folks relocated to Dell, Arkansas. (Dell was a little community about ten miles away from Blytheville, where I grew up.)

Of course, the first thing they built was a church, Dell Baptist Church. John was the first song leader there. My family likes to think we got most of our musical abilities from his part of the family tree. The church is still on the same spot, and I still have extended family there.

John's daughter was my grandmother, Janie Lillian Hardin. She was a poet; one poem she wrote, "That Open Door," described the experience of dying and going to meet the Lord. My family published some of her poems in book form. I like to think I got my poetry talent from her.

Grandmother was one of those ladies who was honestly effervescent. She would sparkle! She was tall, with black hair, high cheekbones, and dark eyes. Even in her later years, she never looked her age. She was not Mrs. Ross to anybody; she was Janie to everybody.

The first grandchild decides what the grandparents will be called. I was the first grandchild, and in my little-girl mind, someone called "Mamaw" was supposed to be a little woman with white hair in a bun. And she wasn't like that. I thought "Grandmother" was the elegant name, so that's what we called her.

Grandmother married James Ross. I called him Daddy Jim. He was a very quiet man, a carpenter by trade. In the 1940s, he built the last house they lived in. Grandmother picked out land just two blocks from the church they went to; since she never learned to drive, she wanted to make sure she could be able to walk around to church.

It was a white frame house, typical of the time. It had a big living room, a dining room, and bedrooms across the back. This house, where I lived from childhood until I married, is the house about which I would later write "This Ole Place" (Ernie Haase & Signature Sound).

Daddy Jim was such a quiet fellow, and my grandmother was the most vivacious lady who ever lived. I asked her once how he won her hand. She said, "He did two things: He made friends with my brother, Jack—and when Daddy would allow suitors to visit, he'd come earlier than anyone else could get there."

Once, Daddy Jim told me that he looked up into the Dell Baptist Church choir one day, saw my Grandmother, and fell in love right then!

They always cooked breakfast together. Daddy Jim would put that old-time coffee pot on, the kind that made coffee on the burner of the stove (*my*, but you can't get coffee that hot anymore!), and Grandmother made biscuits. (My grandmother's biscuits are *still* legendary.) They could both make our Southern-style breakfast gravy and fry the bacon and eggs. They'd visit together before the rest of us got up, then we'd all head for the kitchen for a *feast* every morning! I never went to school with just a bowl of cereal in my little belly in my life!

Grandmother lived an interesting life. Coming through the Depression, you know they didn't have anything. When her family moved out of the deep country into the little farming community of Dell, she taught herself how to fix hair. She would cut people's hair for a quarter or dime, whatever they were able to pay. She took a beauty course in the '40s; at the time she passed it, she was the oldest operator in the state of Arkansas.

She worked at the beauty school for a while. Daddy Jim built an extra room in their house to become a beauty shop, so she could work out of the home. She was self-employed, doing her own bookkeeping and running her own business at a time when very few women did.

Daddy Jim had a mild stroke later in life, and a heart attack took him when he was 67 years old.

My mother, Blanche Ross Branscum, was the oldest of four. Her brothers were Uncle Raymond and Uncle Marvin, and between those two was Aunt Mavis.

There used to be a grocery store in Dell called Brownlee's Grocery. Every Saturday, they'd have a little talent show. I'm not sure what the prizes were—it was hard times, so it couldn't have been much—but Grandmother told me that one of her kids won every single week! My mother, Uncle Raymond, and Aunt Mavis could sing. Aunt Mavis was itty bitty, but she'd recite the longest poems you ever heard. And they'd stand little tiny Marvin, who was seven years younger than Aunt Mavis, up on an orange crate, and he would preach! (Uncle Marvin was like an older brother to me, since I was the first grandchild.)

If Uncle Raymond had been in the right place at the right time, he could have been in the Grand Ole Opry. He could play the guitar and sing like an angel. He looked great in a cowboy hat, sounded a lot like Ernest Tubb or Hank Williams, and had the personality to go with it!

If Aunt Mavis and Mama had been in the right place at the right time, they'd probably have been singing as big band singers, touring with someone like Tommy Dorsey.

No question, Uncle Marvin would've done stand-up comedy. He just had that "special something"!

And consequently, little Dianne just loved to be in front of an audience! She got that early! I've never known stage fright. I think that's because performing just came naturally to my family. My brother Jim says, with a little bit of pride, that there are no wallflowers in my family! That's a nice way to say we're all a bunch of hams, that's what we are!

Daddy's name was Marvin Oliver Branscum, but all his life, he was called "Buster." He had a terrible beginning. His grandparents raised him after his father died. His formal education ended around the third grade, since nobody could send him to school.

He was still in his twenties when he married my mother, but he was married before that. He married really young, and when his first wife had their first baby, the baby died. She got pregnant again, but this time the baby lived, and she died. That baby is my half-sister Shirley, who's three and a half years older than I am. My daddy couldn't take care of a baby by himself, so her grandparents took her.

I don't know how this worked out, but later in my childhood, her grandparents moved right across from us, so we grew up together and all went to Calvary Baptist Church. We sang together when I was a little third grader. She sang melody, and I sang alto; we dressed in our Sunday best and sang at church socials and other events.

My mama said that when my daddy was in the room, you couldn't see anybody else. He was absolutely movie-star gorgeous, and I've got pictures to prove it! He was fun and twinkly-eyed—full of the stuff!

When Daddy was in the army, they would make you run miles holding up your rifles, for no good reason. One day, when they got back to the post, all those poor little boys' tongues were hanging out, and they were just about ready to drop. My daddy was nearly dead, too, but right at the end, he did a little buck-dance jig, just to prove to everybody that he could! He probably went in and just about died on the bed! How they laughed about that! A little jig just to show the brass that you can't walk a Branscum so hard that he can't still dance a jig!

My parents were fabulous dancers, back when the jitterbug was the rage. I was conceived when he was stationed in Corvallis, Oregon, which Mama said was the prettiest place she ever saw.

Back then, they had jitterbug contests at huge armories; hundreds and hundreds of servicemen would dance. One time, General Patton and his wife were guests at an event like that. The last couple standing was the winner, and my mother and daddy won the trophy! And as part of the prize, she got to dance with General Patton, and he got to dance with the general's wife. Mama said, "He was tall and impressive, but he couldn't dance like your daddy!"

My daddy was a casualty of World War II, pure and simple. He was at the Battle of the Bulge. He was a medic, and they didn't let the medics carry a weapon. But they did let him carry what was left of his friends on stretchers off of the battlefield. I don't care who you are—that just does something to you. My daddy was never the same again.

I believe he had what we now know as Post-Traumatic Stress Disorder, and nobody knew how to deal with it back in those days. People had to medicate with something, and he started drinking. He never drank anything but Coca-Cola before he went over; my mother wouldn't have married a man who drank alcohol. That was back in the '40s, before there was any Alcoholics Anonymous or any help for alcoholics like that. My mother described it this way: "My husband went overseas. And somebody came home who looked like him, but wasn't him. He was never totally like himself again."

He was never able to overcome it in time to save the marriage, so my home was a casualty of the war. He moved to Detroit and disappeared from our lives. He told Mama that if he was ever able to stay sober, he'd like to be a part of our lives—and if not, he didn't want us to know him that way. He was never able to get sober his whole life long.

His life started and ended unhappily. He knew real happiness before the war years, but after the divorce, I don't believe he was ever happy again. Daddy went to his grave in love with my mother.

2

I was born when my daddy was in the war. Mama took me to Olan Mills® every month to get my picture made, so he could see the progress of his little girl. I was a little bigger than a toddler the first time he got to see me face-to-face.

When my parents learned I was on the way, they were happy; my mother said that the happiest days she ever had were when she was carrying me. But that was the end of the happiness they were ever able to have together. When she was carrying my little brother, she cried every day, because she already knew how things were going to be.

Mama had a terrible time delivering Jim. She lost a lot of blood, and back then, I don't think they knew the long-term effects of that. She was so weak that there were days when she couldn't stay on her feet long enough to fix his bottle.

She taught me how to pull the kitchen chair over to the stove, heat his bottle, and feed him. So I thought he was *mine*! It was like I had my own doll, a big ol' beautiful baby with just a tiny bit of blond hair and big ol' black eyes—cute as a button! I was maternal about him then, and I've always been; even though now he's a big ol' strappin' prince among preachers, in my mind, he's still my little brother.

He was a colicky little baby. Even babies know when there's stress in a home. But once we moved to Grandmother's, that little ol' thing started eating like a little pig and got all chubby and happy. He has been a joy to me all his life!

My mama was a homemaker until the divorce. Then she had to go to bookkeeping school to learn how to support herself. She had a brilliant mind and passed the course with flying colors!

She found a job at Planter's Hardware in Blytheville. Jim was still just a baby, so Grandmother hired a lady to help in the house and watch after us, so she could work in the beauty shop.

Mama's first day of work was so sad. We couldn't wrap our minds around the fact that she was going off in the day-time, away from us. She had never been away from us in our lives. Since we lived one block off of Main Street in Blytheville, Mama only had to walk up the block to catch the city bus. Jim and I stood there in Grandmother's yard, crying, waving, and watching Mama walk away.

In a normal situation, Mama would have been a perfect wife. She was a marvelous cook and could sew dresses for me without a pattern. We would have had the perfect post-war

1950s little house somewhere. Daddy might have gotten in church and all might have been well. We will never know.

Aunt Mavis, my mother's sister, also married a military man. They had one daughter, Lilli Ann. He had his own private battles, and the marriage never did work out. Back then, there wasn't anywhere else for a divorced woman to go but to her parents' house.

So there we were. All of a sudden, my grandmother had two daughters and three grandkids back in her home.

Looking back now, I know what she saw. She saw three little kids who didn't have a daddy anymore, and who anybody would say were behind the eight ball. *Nobody* was divorced in the '50s, but both her daughters were.

I know that she absolutely determined in her heart, "These children are going to be as happy as I can make them. They're going to have a start. They're going to have a good life, 'cause I'm going to make that happen."

Grandmother saw to it that we were always in church. She saw to it that Lilli Ann and I had piano lessons. And she made everything a fun adventure. She was the greatest storyteller that ever was. She was wise and strong in spirit. She never made anything look like "Oh, poor me, I'm being imposed on. My home's been taken over by children; what am I going to do?" Never that!

We thought the sun rose and set on her. She was everything secure in our lives; it's like nothing could harm us if Grandmother was there. Nothing!

We had one bathroom at that house, with a tub but no shower. We had a lot of bedrooms, but a two or three bathroom home didn't exist back then.

One afternoon, I came home after school crying. The next day, I had to have a shower cap in my locker to get my grade in Physical Education, but it was too late to purchase one.

Well, Grandmother went back behind a little closet in her beauty shop. She came out and produced . . . a shower cap!

I said, "What are you doin' with a shower cap? We don't have a shower!"

She just smiled! This is how she was, so help me! Whatever you needed, Grandmother had. Always!

Whatever Jim, Lilli, and I thought was a great idea, Grandmother thought was a great idea. I came to her one day and asked her to give my hair permanent waves. I had naturally curly hair, so I didn't need a permanent, but I thought it would be a cool thing to do!

I said, "Grandmother, would you give me a permanent?"

She said, "Well, sure!"

After she was done, I looked like Buckwheat from the *Little Rascals*!

One day, Jim asked Grandmother to give him a mohawk. She said, "I sure will!" She got that razor out, and she cut that kid a mohawk!

When Mama came home, she almost got the vapors—and she *never* got the vapors. She said, "Oh, my goodness! What did you do?"

Of course, Grandmother had the last word. She said, "It'll grow out; it's no big deal."

I know now what it was. She did what little things she could do for us. She just was *not* going to make us feel like victims. She was going to make our lives good if she could.

She just did whatever had to be done, and never made it look hard, never made anybody feel like they were in the way.

Grandmother had a heart attack in 1976 at age 72. Talk about someone's world coming all the way out from under them —I didn't think I could draw another breath.

She lived in the hospital for six weeks before she died. Her friends came out begging to see her. Her customers, friends from organizations she was in, the neighbor ladies, the church ladies all came. Everybody loved her! Her doctor wouldn't let any of them visit her because he wanted to keep her quiet. In retrospect, knowing she was going to die anyway, we probably would have overridden that.

Grandmother was a Bible teacher extraordinaire. She was the most wonderful Sunday School teacher I ever knew; I sat under her teaching for years. I absolutely know that's where Jim, Lilli, and I all got our teaching gift. Lilli is a kindergarten teacher at a Presbyterian academy, teaching little kids about Jesus. My brother is a Southern Baptist pastor. I teach Sunday School. I know we got those skills from her.

If we had lived a regular life with Mama and Daddy, I have no idea what my brother and I would be today—especially if Daddy had been drinking. But God in His wisdom put us in the home of Janie Ross and under her influence. He made her my grandmother. I didn't see God's plan at the time, but I look back and say, "Lord, I see so plainly how you did it."

When I was in grade school, music was a required subject. One lady in Blytheville, Mrs. Ralph Berryman, rotated between the three grade schools in our town, teaching children to read music. Every spring she had a big program. She brought all the schools together on the football field, putting musical kids like me out on the front, letting us do little leading parts.

When I was in seventh grade, I was in a glee club. Somehow my choir teacher figured out that I instinctively knew the scale. Even though I didn't know what to call it, I knew what a third interval was. She put me in front of the class when she was showing the intervals in a chord, saying, "Now Dianne, can you sing this one before I play it?" And I could; my love for harmony just developed early!

It's so easy to look back and see how God used it all—He gave me the gifts first of all, and then He put me in the situation that it took to hone them and make sure they blossomed.

When I was a little grade school girl, I went forward at a revival meeting. The evangelist preached a graphic sermon on Hell, and I was terrified—my little knees were knocking together. I don't suppose I will ever know how much my decision to go forward was conviction or just terror.

I went to the altar and shook hands with the evangelist; that I remember. They stood me up on the communion table in my little frilly dress. I remember that, and I remember people shaking my hand.

I remember everything but praying the sinner's prayer.

3

Mama and Aunt Mavis formed a trio called the Ross Sisters in the early 1950s, with a friend of theirs, Emma Shook. (They originally called themselves the Harmonettes.) Emma was dark-haired and had a really pretty alto voice. She was a great gal and lots of fun.

When she stopped singing with the group, they hired Lavelle Jones. Her face reminded me a lot of Doris Day, and she really had a great voice in the high range. When she started with them, she could almost read their lips, so she wouldn't have to look on a page of paper. She sang for several years with them.

They started singing all around our area. We went to hear the Goss Brothers and the Rangers, groups which sang those difficult vocal arrangements, so I learned to love all that when I was a kid.

The Ross Sisters sang just about every weekend, all over upper Arkansas and the Missouri boot-heel, occasionally over in Kentucky or West Tennessee.

I didn't sing with them that much around home when Lavelle was singing with them. But, when I was twelve, she moved on. Mama and Aunt Mavis must have known I could sing. I didn't try out, and I don't remember a conversation where they came and said, "Guess what, you're in the trio." I sang the high part (which they called the tenor). Mama sang lead, and Aunt Mavis sang alto.

Aunt Mavis had always played piano for the Ross Sisters. Grandmother had seen me watch her playing the piano and knew that I wanted to play just like her! So when I was just a grade schooler, about eight or nine years old, Grandmother sent me to my first piano lessons.

My teacher, Jack Tapp, was an old-style quartet pianist from our church. When he played hymns, he played an open-handed style, putting in all the fills. I could look at his hands, see what he was doing, and do it myself. So, when I started playing piano, I used the chording style that the piano players used when the piano was all that you had. Hovie Lister, Wally Varner, and all the other piano players of the day made their own percussion. Nowadays, you've got the bass going, the other instruments, et cetera. But not back then; it was piano only!

So when I joined the Ross Sisters, I started playing the piano, freeing Aunt Mavis to focus on her emceeing.

We had a 15 minute live radio show at 9:15 every Sunday morning on KLCN in Blytheville, which was a *very* strong radio station which could be heard a *long* way off. Some of the biggest acts of the 1940s and 1950s sang on that station.

We had no records to sell and didn't own any P.A. equipment. All we cared about was where we would sing and what time, what we would wear (we dressed alike), and what songs we would sing on our program.

Mind again, I was the first grandchild. Since I was twelve years old and they had put me in the trio, I became like another one of the sisters. I actually became pretty sophisticated. I was dressing like them, wearing high-heel shoes like them, and going where they went. I could talk like an adult, and actually pretend to more sophistication than I had!

In fact, just after I started with the Ross Sisters, a very young and very single Jim Hamill tried to date me! We were booked somewhere in Memphis; Jim's dad was pastor of the big First Assembly Church there at the time. Jim was probably about 20 or so, and he was singing with a local quartet who was on the program. He was a masterful singer even *then*.

Of course, I was dressed up just like Mama and Aunt Mavis. He got to visiting with me with a twinkle in his eye, and I thought he was cute, so I was visiting, too. Afterward, he went over to Mama, and said, "Hey, do you know what y'all's piano player told me? She told me she was 12 years old and that you are her mama!" Obviously, he didn't believe me and thought he was getting the brush-off—I looked *so* grown up!

My mother looked at him without smiling and said, "She *is* twelve years old, and I *am* her mama." Then he laughed, and she did, too.

Early on, I just felt like an adult. Even though I enjoyed my school friends, I was always more comfortable with people older than I was. When I started dating, I didn't have a bit of time for a boy my own age—I thought that was way beneath me!

My family helped start the Ridgecrest Baptist Church in Blytheville in 1957. I was already playing for the Ross Sisters, and I became the church pianist. By the grace of God, I've been a church musician ever since.

I started teaching Sunday School—small children—there when I was in high school. (I have taught it ever since.) My mother was a member there to the end of her life.

Smilin' Joe Roper of the Melody Boys Quartet encouraged Mama and Aunt Mavis to start their trio. He knew they could sing, and he would let them open up at some of the Melody Boys' singings. So that group was instrumental in letting the Ross Sisters get somewhere back in those days.

I wanted to play just like Smilin' Joe; he had a touch like nobody else. And the Melody Boys had a marvelous blend. They had a lead singer named Fred Smith, who had a little bit of a Jake Hess type voice, but without the stylistic way that Jake sang. Jerry Venable was singing tenor at the time. Coolidge Faulkner was singing baritone. Gerald Williams, who led the group in later years, was a teenager, singing bass. Over the years, the personnel changed. But to hear them sing, and to hear Joe play, was just amazing. And since we lived in Arkansas, they came up around our way a lot.

Smilin' Joe had a dry sense of humor. He didn't smile; that was the joke. But his kind of comedy included a Victor Borge routine. Victor was a comedian who played piano back in the '40s and '50s. He played the piano with a punctuated style of dots as part of a dialogue he was doing. It was a funny act, and Joe could do the very same thing.

Joe was an encourager all the way through. One time, the Ross Sisters were booked on the Arkansas State Singing Convention. It was going to be the biggest crowd we'd had. I was twelve or thirteen and really nervous.

It wasn't a church; it was a big auditorium. I had never experienced stage fright, but I did that day. Joe sat me down backstage and talked to me. He told me that I wasn't supposed to be afraid of anything. I was supposed to get right up there and sing like I always did, that I was going to do great, and not to worry. I never had to be afraid when I was playing God's music. He helped me so much that day.

When we got to the '60s, I wanted to play just like Henry Slaughter from the Imperials, and I actually learned a few good licks from him. Then I discovered Eddie Crook, playing for the Happy Goodmans, and all I wanted out of life was to play just like Eddie Crook! But Joe was my first piano hero.

I never will forget the first time we heard the Goodmans sing "Who Am I." We were just knocked out by that song. Back then (as I wish it was now), you could walk to the group's product table. They had a rack of sheet music of every song they were doing; you could buy the two or three page sheet music for a dollar.

Before they even got to the end of the song, I slipped out and went to the lobby of the Ellis Auditorium in Memphis, and bought that sheet music, because I was afraid they'd sell out of it and we wouldn't have it! We learned that song—the arrangement and the parts—driving home from Memphis!

As little as I was, I remember the Blackwood Brothers when R.W. Blackwood and Bill Lyles were still with them. (They died in a 1954 plane crash.)

Bill Lyles used to keep a hymnal tucked up under his arm when he was on stage. Oh, what a bass singer! J.D. was low, but he didn't have the tone that Bill Lyles had!

And R.W. was just the one you watched. He was just the funniest thing; he was as cute as he could be—he was the jokester. He was the one that was full of fun and had such a distinctive baritone voice.

I remember watching the Godfrey Show the night they won. They sang "Have You Talked to the Man Upstairs." It was hands-down—there wasn't any question among those contestants that night who was going to win. They electrified that audience.

But quartets back in those days could have electrified audiences in Las Vegas! They just could. Back in those days, there were pop music quartets like the Four Aces and the Ames Brothers. Other acts had a full orchestra on stage. If all you had was a piano, you had to have the vocal chops, because there wasn't anything to cover up what you couldn't do well! But the Statesmen and Blackwoods electrified everybody.

Nobody could sing like our folks! Barbershop has a sweet sound, but it doesn't have a Gospel quartet's excitement and chemistry.

I think that the most hardened atheist, if he had a musician's ear and heard the best of our quartets—if he listened to the singing, with the harmonies and the chords, I think it would knock his socks off.

Mama and Aunt Mavis took me to the first National Quartet Convention at the Ellis Auditorium in Memphis in 1957. It was exciting, because it included all the major groups at the time. I don't think anyone knew then how long it would last, or what it would become. The auditorium had two separate sections, with a stage in the middle. Groups had to turn back and forth, to work both sides.

Quartet Convention closed out with a Sunday morning worship service with Statesmen pianist Hovie Lister preaching. He would preach his hair down! He'd get his sleeves pushed up, kinda like the preacher I wrote about in "He Said"! I never got to hear him preach in that setting because we didn't stay for the Sunday service. (We played for church and had the radio program.)

My little town was close to Memphis, so proximity allowed me the privilege of being able to hear those groups.

I was at the National Quartet Convention the first night the Rambos ever sang. They didn't sound like anybody else. Everyone else was diction-conscious; you know how the diction was in those days, with groups like the Weatherfords and the Rangers. Here came folks who said Hea-VUHN, and "there's no stars in the skies." It's not grammatically correct, but Dottie Rambo didn't even know. It didn't even matter, because it was so gorgeous!

They were just raw and untrained, and had electrifying harmonies. They didn't *look* like anybody else, and they didn't *sound* like anybody else. They changed everything. They became huge—as much for the way they sounded as for Dottie's writing.

As good as it was, it took a while for her writing to come to the forefront. Early on, the big news was that they were just so different from what had been on the stage before in a male-dominated business. Eva Mae, Mom Speer, Mama Klaudt, and the Chuck Wagon Gang ladies were pretty much the only ladies in the business, and they were only there because they were married to the men in the group!

If you took Buck on his own, he wasn't a great singer. But he had the perfect blend with Dottie and Reba. It was the most amazing blend. And if you heard Dottie sing by herself, you wouldn't think she'd sound good with Reba and Buck! But she did! I wanted to sing just like her. My little reedy second soprano wasn't anywhere close, but I wanted to sing like Dottie so bad. Nobody could!

I didn't really know her in those days, and I didn't get acquainted with her until she finally got through the worst of her health problems. In the last few years of her life, she got well enough to do a little touring. She told me one time, "If you're writin' for the Lord, the Devil will fight you tooth and nail. He'll do everything he can to slap you down and keep you down." But he couldn't stop her! She was just as great on her last day as she was on her first. She never slipped. I'll always miss Dottie Rambo.

When I was singing with the Ross Sisters, we would learn our arrangements in the car. We would learn the modulations and swap parts as needed. For years, I thought that everyone who could sing could harmonize and swap parts; I didn't know there were people who could really sing well, but could only sing the lead.

When Elvis was living in Memphis, he went over to First Assembly to try out with the Songfellows. They loved his voice, but he couldn't hear the baritone part, and that was the available part. I've always grieved because of that, because I've always thought that if he'd been in our music, we'd still have him. He'd be playing with his grandkids and probably still singing with a quartet somewhere.

He was a little Pentecostal boy who went to the First Assembly with his parents. He had the deepest church background, and he always loved Gospel music best!

I actually saw Elvis before he ever got famous. He was touring the high schools in the South. Mama took me to a concert at the high school in Leachville, Arkansas, a little farming community between Blytheville and Jonesboro. We sat up in the bleachers in the gymnasium to hear whoever came on. Well, out came Elvis, with guitarist Scotty Moore and bassist Bill Black, barreling out there, just those three. He didn't have his own record deal yet, so he was singing other artists' hits. I'm tellin' you, he electrified that crowd. I bought the 8x10 glossy of him. He was sittin' on the bench in the gym, signin' those pictures; I filed by, and he signed my picture, which I still have.

Even after he got to be "ELVIS," he still loved Gospel Music. At Quartet Convention, they would spirit Elvis into a little room the size of a broom closet just off the stage, where he could hear the singing, but nobody could see him.

One year, Mama and Aunt Mavis went with a couple of friends. (I wasn't with them this time.) They were going backstage to speak with someone that they knew, and one of the gals got separated from the others. She opened the door to that little room, by accident, and there he sat!

Her mouth was already open, making a giant O.

He said, "Oh please, lady, please, just please don't say anything. If they find out…" She was really so shocked, I don't know if she could have made a sound anyway! Mama said she just started backing out like she'd seen a ghost! She almost fainted!

That's how the poor little fella had to hear Gospel singing in his hometown; they had to hide him!

Toward the end of the 1960s, the Ross Sisters made our only official studio recording. One side of the record featured Reverend Paul Kirkendall telling the testimony of his conversion. He was a dynamic preacher who opened the Mississippi County Union Mission, a local mission for vagrant men. The other side featured one song each from key people who had sung a lot at the mission, and had a heart for that ministry. We sang "Pass Me Not."

Brother Paul was a colorful character. Before his conversion, he was known in town as the local gangster. The rumor was that he had organized crime connections, perhaps like lower-level Mafia. He ran a place called "The Puff" on Main Street in Blytheville. It seemed like a pool hall in front, but heavyweight gambling and all kinds of illegal activities were going on in the back. In other words, he was a rough customer.

He was married to a godly lady who always tried to get him to go to church. He never did want to go. Finally, one Sunday, she convinced him to go to church. She was a Baptist, so they were going to Trinity Baptist Church, which was across the street from the Pentecostal church. The story he told in his testimony was that the Baptist Church parking lot was full at the time. Brother Paul said, "I was lost, but I had enough conscience to think it would be wrong to park in the Pentecost church lot, and walk across to the Baptist church. So I told my wife, if we're gonna park at this Pentecost church, we're goin' in this Pentecost church!" His wife was so glad that she didn't care!

Brother Paul came under conviction in the service. He'd never had been around church, and the way he put it was, "I didn't know John 3:16 from an algebra equation!" But he walked up front, shook hands with the pastor, prayed the sinner's prayer, and was saved. His words were, "Jesus, I will trust You."

In his mission, he took in the vagrant men, the men we call homeless today. He'd give them a place to sleep, feed them, and find jobs for them. He would have worship services for those men, and anybody else who wanted to come. He was legendary for being able to get people to come up there and sing. Everybody loved him and knew his testimony, and the bottom line was, you couldn't tell him no! He just didn't take no!

The Ross Sisters sang there a lot, and other people in our town did, too. Someone had the idea to make that recording; we were one of the groups who came in and got in on that session. We played and sang it through one time, and got it the first time! Some of our other friends who didn't sing as often were kinda nervous, but we were old hands by then. I was in my early twenties, and I'd been doin' it since I was twelve years old!

In a great sense, the '60s were a continuation of the '50s. I was still singing with my family and playing piano for church services.

As I got into high school, I did play with a rock-and-roll band. We didn't play in joints and dives; we played in wholesome places, like the air base and community centers. I didn't see any conflict in that. I was just a kid, and I loved it all. On Saturday nights, I was either playing with the band or singing with the Ross Sisters somewhere! I lived a schizophrenic life of loving rock-and-roll music, but always loving church music and Gospel music better.

All of the music I loved growing up, including what my mother taught me from the big bands, influenced my writing style. I just loved Ray Charles and Jerry Lee Lewis. I loved rhythm and blues. I loved Mahalia Jackson and Black Gospel like it was then, with the choirs. I loved the great hymns, and I loved church music. And, of course, I loved Gospel Music.

You have to bear in mind, I was thinking I was saved as a little girl, and I wasn't. Through these years, I was a good girl, and I was a well-behaved girl, but I wasn't a saved girl. Maybe if I had been a saved girl, it would've dawned on me, "I probably shouldn't play for a rock-and-roll band on Saturday night and for the Baptist Church on Sunday morning!"

I loved the Lord in the way an unsaved person could, and I loved the Bible. I can't explain it, but the Lord gave me some understanding of those things. He knew He had a calling on me, and He knew that He had to prepare me when I was young.

4

My cousin Lilli Ann was the first one to leave the nest. A young man from Dell, Arkansas, was courting her during her high school years; he was determined to marry her the minute she got out of high school. She did marry him and moved away in 1968.

My brother Jim joined the army and went to Vietnam. He had fallen in love with a young lady named Sondra before he went. They married in 1970, when he got back.

When I graduated from high school at the age of seventeen, I had no intention of going to college. Back then, there were two kinds of girls who went to college—the ones who wanted to teach school and the ones who wanted to marry a college man. I didn't want to get married nearly that soon! I wanted to get a job and to buy a car and some great clothes! That was my plan, and that's exactly what I did!

I went to work for the telephone company, Southwestern Bell, the Monday after I graduated from high school. Now I was a seventeen-year-old kid, but I wasn't an operator. I got a job as a service representative in the business office; I was selling telephones, calling people, and collecting bills.

I made $50 per week—a lot of money in 1962! Nobody my age had that kind of money in their hands! I thought, "What am I going to do with all this money?" So I bought a little 1962 ivory-colored Comet with red bucket seats. That's a girl car, I'm telling you!

I stayed single for ten years, working and performing music. It was a great time.

In 1969, Aunt Mavis moved to Texas. That left Mama and me with nobody to sing with, until I met Tim Wilkinson.

When I first met him, I was engaged to his roommate, Matt. Matt and Tim were medics at the Air Force base hospital, and I was in Civil Service there. (Civil Service was the was the best job in Blytheville at the time.) At the hospital, I *was* medical records. They had a huge outpatient area, but there was a little twenty-five-bed medical/surgical area.

I had never met Tim because he worked the night shift in the Air Force base hospital. Matt had a 8x10 picture of me in their room that Tim saw all the time, but he didn't know me.

Tim knew what I looked like from that picture. One time I came out to the hospital in the evening for something. A friend and I were going to a party, and I wanted to run into the hospital to pick up something that I had left in my office. Of course, I was dressed up. Tim told me later that he saw me walk by, and he knew it was me because of the picture!

Tim and I did finally meet, and really started out as friends early on. Matt and I eventually broke up, but I stayed friends with Tim. We would go to singings together. He was different from the others I went with because he went to church with me, and the rest never did.

Tim loved Gospel music, though he had never been to a singing before. He was from Oklahoma; he watched the Gospel Singing Jubilee and was a huge Happy Goodmans fan. So I took him to the Quartet Convention the last year that it was in Memphis. They always ask everybody at the beginning to stand up and sing "Amazing Grace." When we did, I thought, "This guy can sing!"

I had good seats for us; we were not very many rows from the stage. When the Imperials, who were backing Elvis up at the time, finished their stand, Elvis came out from behind the velvet curtain and saluted them. Tim, who was a big Elvis fan, almost strangled me, trying to get his hands on the binoculars!

Tim really wanted to hear me play the piano. So he came to the house one night, and I'll never forget the first thing I did. I played Dottie Rambo's "The Holy Hills of Heaven Call Me." Well, he knew that song, so he started singing it. Mama wandered over and found a harmony part; then I joined in.

Tim had never sung outside his home or car in his life. But I already knew he had a really, really good voice. As it turned out, the three of us blended well together.

At first, Tim had trouble hearing a harmony part, but he got to where he could hear a part pretty well. He couldn't read music. (Mama, Aunt Mavis, and Jim didn't either, but harmony came easily to all of them.) If he ever learned a harmony part, he never lost it. But most of the time he sang lead, because he had a good lead voice.

We always had a monthly singing convention in Blytheville. It rotated between different churches, and people were used to the Ross Sisters always singing there.

I don't remember the golden occasion, but one time, when we had practiced enough, Mama and I got up and got Tim up there. It sounded good. After we did that another time or two, people said, "We're not goin' to be able to call y'all the Ross Sisters anymore! You're just going to have to come up with some other kind of name!" So we called ourselves the Revelations.

We didn't do a lot of singing then because Tim got out of the Air Force in about 1970 and moved to Memphis. He went to work at St. Jude Hospital at that time. We'd still call each other pretty often, but he wasn't able to get to Blytheville much.

At some point, Tim came a-courting for real. I was dating somebody else. I think he decided, "If I'm ever going to get this done, I'm going to have to shoot him out of the saddle to get in here and make my pitch!" Of course, he had more charm than the law should allow, and he could wrap my mother and grandmother around his finger!

When he'd come up to visit—well, who else would come and take me out on a date? Nobody!

So it just developed from a friendship into a romantic relationship. We began to talk about getting married, and we were talking about dates and making plans. But I don't remember exactly when he said, "Will you marry me?"

In an Air Force town, you can have a different boyfriend every day if you want to! The airbase is full of boys who are away from home and lonesome!

I would be dating a guy, and he would fall in love. Sometimes I would say I was, when I was really just kind of in *like*! But I wasn't lying at the time! Sometimes I was in love with *love*.

The make or break for every one of those situations was: Am I willing to move away to wherever this guy lives and go off and leave my grandmother? The answer was always no!

So when I was talking about getting married to Tim, Grandmother said to me, "Why are you letting them give you all these wedding showers? You know you're not going through with this one, either—you never do!"

You see, I liked being single! I was still living at home, Grandmother was there, Mama was there, I was there. We were like three gals in a boarding-house. I had a great life. But by the time you get to be twenty-seven, there's just not a lot of cool guys out there anymore. They're all married! So I decided, "Okay, if you're ever going to get serious about this thing, you'd better decide to settle down with somebody!"

She said, "You won't marry him!"

I said, "Yes, I am, Grandmother, I'm going to marry this one. We're going to live our lives singin' for the Lord, we're going to do church work, and we're going to do God's work. That's what Tim and I are going to do."

Now I hadn't told Tim that! I hadn't asked God! That was *my* idea!

At the time when we were getting ready to get married, I wore a size sixteen. They just didn't make the kind of wedding dress I wanted for that size. I had heard about a Turkish girl, an Air Force wife, who knew how to sew without a pattern. You could bring her two or three magazine pictures of bridal gowns, and perhaps something you drew, and tell her what you wanted the composite to be. And she could do it! So I designed my wedding dress and veil, and she had it made up.

I had three bridesmaids. One of them was my cousin, Lilli Ann. She is about 5'10½" in her stocking feet. (Her mother, my mother, and our grandmother were all tall. At 5'4½", I'm considered short in my family!) The second was a gal I worked with at the base hospital, an Air Force nurse. She was tiny, perhaps 4'11"! The third, who worked with me at base supply and was my best friend at the time, was rather on the heavy side.

I couldn't find bridesmaid dresses for these women!

I wanted my color to be pink. We found some beautiful dresses that were pink. And this is how my grandmother could make something out of nothing: We got the dress sizes as close as we could. She was able to cut off enough of the tall girl's dress to build it into the side of the heavy girl's dress. And so help me, when the girls all lined up, it looked like their dresses were tailor-made!

We were married on March 11, 1972 at Ridgecrest Baptist Church, which my grandparents had helped found, and where I grew up. Since my daddy was out of my life after I was five, Uncle Raymond gave me away. Of course, Tim's folks were there, and his best friend came from Oklahoma to be his best man. It was a beautiful wedding.

Tim didn't sing to me and I didn't sing to him. A gal in Blytheville who played often at the singing conventions played the organ, and a classmate of mine with a beautiful soprano voice sang "My Own True Love" from *Gone With the Wind*, and one of my favorite hymns, "Oh Perfect Love."

We didn't really have a big honeymoon. Since we were both working, we spent the weekend in Memphis, came back, and went to work!

We moved into a little furnished rental. It was small, but plenty for what we needed. I think the rent was something like $65 per month. (It was ridiculously cheaper to live then!)

We didn't have any furniture of our own. I came in one day, and there was an upright Baldwin piano sitting in the living room. Tim absolutely loved piano playing and always loved to hear me play.

I said, "What have you done?"

He said, "Well, we don't have to keep it. I thought it was so pretty, and I wanted to hear you play it." He got it on approval; if, after a couple of months, we decided we didn't want it, they'd come and get it, no harm, no foul.

We didn't have a refrigerator to our name, or anything else that was ours, but we had a piano! It was a Baldwin Acrosonic, and it had a marvelous touch and a wonderful sound. Of course, we kept it! The songs I wrote after we married were written at that piano, or that was the first thing I played them on. It turned out to be a really good investment.

Tim went to work at the local hospital, Chickasawba Hospital. He worked in the emergency department as a paramedic, and eventually became the director of the emergency department.

I was working the Civil Service at the Air Force base. I got a promotion from base supply to the hospital. It was actually a big facility, but most of it was outpatient. I did everything that had to do with medical records—I literally was the medical records department.

Later on, the Chickasawba Hospital administrator offered me a job as Director of Medical Records. He offered to pay for my credential, with what is now the American Health Information Management Association. (At that time you could get it by correspondence course.) I took that job, so Tim and I were both working at that hospital through the '70s.

When we married, Tim was already going to my home church. I was still playing piano. The day came when all the men who led singing had either left or moved away, and one day, we just didn't have anyone. Someone asked Tim if he would lead the singing, so he began to do that. He had a good, loud voice, and people could hear him.

Unlike a minister of music, a song leader is off the cuff. He doesn't move his arms; he just stands up there and calls the number. Tim was self-taught, but he could get more out of a choir than anybody I ever heard who wasn't a professional. And so, for the rest of his life, we had a church ministry together. He was the choir director, and I played piano.

After Tim went to work at the local hospital and things really settled down, my mother, Tim, and I started singing more often. When my brother Jim got back from Vietnam, he joined us, and we sang quite a bit through the '70s.

When it was the Ross Sisters, we just had fun singing. We didn't have to worry about overhead, since we didn't have any overhead! We didn't have any equipment, trailers, or records to sell. All we had were the flashy clothes on our back! We just showed up! If they had microphones, we used them, and if they didn't, we didn't! We'd just get in the car, go sing, and have a good, good time!

It wasn't quite the same when we got those boys in the group! Tim and Jim wanted the trailer, the record table, and records to sell. But it was good; we sold enough records to make a second, and enough of that one to pay for the trailer!

Our first record was called *Behold the Lamb*. It had a gold and white cover with a cross, and our picture on the back. I wrote the title cut and another song called "Could This Be the Day?" Joe Kelsey of the Songmasters Quartet, who later recorded "Behold the Lamb," wrote the liner notes.

We recorded both of our albums at Kennett Sound Studios in Kennett, Missouri. Joe Keene ran the sound board; he had a great musician's ear. The bass guitarist on both was Chris Campbell, son of the legendary songwriter Jack Campbell. Tony Bezelle played drums. Dennis Helton was the rhythm guitarist on the second album. And I played piano.

Back then, you sang and played the whole thing through. If you made a mistake, you started over. Before the singers came in, Joe had us musicians in the studio, to see what we could do. I remember thinking, "I don't care if my family ever comes in! This is too much fun!"

The second record was *In the Light of His Coming*. My brother actually had two songs on it, "Then You'll Remember" and "I'm So Glad." My mother, who could also write, had a song on there as well. I had two on this one, "Behold the Bridegroom Cometh" and "Would You Believe It?" We used the latter at invitation time in our programs; it asks the lost person, "Would you believe that somebody loves you enough to die for you?"

For the cover photo, we found a yard in Blytheville where the dogwoods were in bright bloom. The owners let us take our picture in front of the dogwoods.

This was in the later '70s, and for some reason, it was really popular to wear long, casual dresses. Long dresses! All the gals at singings would sing in those long dresses. Almost every group had somebody who could sew; in our case, it was Mama. Everybody had the same pattern, so everybody had the same dress on—it was just the material that was different!

We had the greatest time on the road, but it just got hard. There's nothing in the world as hard as working full time and touring on the weekends, especially when you have committed not to miss church. You have no down time! It just took a toll.

I was always on Weight Watchers® back then. There were nights when I didn't get my supper till two o'clock in the morning; that was just awful. And I was working full time, and I had a full complement of church work.

Everybody would say, "Dianne, it must not be hard for you —you don't have any kids!"

And I'm thinking, "It must not be what? If I wasn't young, I'd already be dead!"

We had to give up traveling in the late '70s. Jim and Sondra were getting ready to start a family, and we had all decided we were never going to let the singing take us away from church. Mama was the church clerk and treasurer. Tim and I did the music, I always taught Sunday School, and Jim had surrendered to the call to preach. It got really, really hard to work all week, sing on Friday and Saturday nights, do church, and go on back to work on Monday.

Honestly, I missed it a little bit, but it was so hard, I was kind of glad to give it up! I loved it when I was younger, but I sure wouldn't have wanted to do it full time. I liked my own nest at home. I liked my own kitchen, I liked my own bed, and I liked my own vanity area! I wouldn't have made a good bus traveler.

I get a lot of requests for songs from weekend warrior groups. I send songs to every single one who ever asks me. I want to make sure they don't ever get the feeling that I'm only interested in the Kingdom Heirs, Triumphant Quartet, and Legacy Five. I don't only send them songs; I have a heart for them because I have lived their life.

I get my performance fix out of playing for church, and occasionally singing there, and that's plenty for me.

5

Even as a little girl, I had always made up verses. I became serious about writing Gospel music when I was in my twenties.

Right at the same time, the Lord really moved me into the Word of God in a serious way. I would come home from work, hole up in my bedroom, and study a couple of commentaries that really opened up the Bible to me.

The commentary that meant the most to me was Clarence Larkin's *Dispensational Truth*. No Christian's library is complete without it.

I was in Civil Service at the time. A co-worker, Staff Sergeant John Hennick, gave me his copy of the book one day. He was a lay preacher. One day he came to me with that book, and he said, "You can have this." I think back; what in the world made him give me his copy? He loved that book! We hadn't known each other that long. It just had to be Providence.

That book changed my life; it opened my Bible up for me. I was absolutely flabbergasted by what I was learning. I didn't know what God was preparing me for; I just knew I couldn't put my Bible down!

Growing up, I hadn't heard the deep things of the Bible. I've talked to many people my age who didn't; perhaps preachers then thought people weren't ready for that. I hadn't heard a lot of preaching about Revelation.

I don't know that I would have ever gone there to that extent or learned what I learned about it, if I hadn't gotten hold of that book. It made me hunger to go deeper and to study more—and it made me want to write.

So I began to write. Early on, it was neither songs or sermons—all I can call it is themes. I wanted to translate what I was learning into my own words. As I began to learn more, it was a small leap to begin to write songs.

I should replace that copy of *Dispensational Truth*, because it's ragged now, the pages are loose, and some of the pages are ripped. But I don't want a new one! I want that one, because it's dear to me! It's one of those things that I pack in my bags when the storm warnings come, along with other things I treasure.

I continued to be in church this whole time—by choice! I became a church musician at age twelve. I taught Sunday School and got married. I was already writing songs that lined up with the Book.

I loved the Lord the only way a lost person can love Him. I loved the things of God. I was right up to the doorway of salvation.

But I was lost.

One night in March 1974, Tim and I were on our way home from church. For some reason, he was in his little yellow truck, and I was in the car. I don't remember why we were in separate vehicles.

I don't know what I was thinking about or what was preached. I could just as well have been coming out of J. C. Penney, or anywhere else, because nothing about the sermon was on my mind. But in what was louder than an audible voice to me, I heard two words.

"You're lost."

I can't explain the cold feeling I had. I knew it was God.

I began to turn over in my mind, "This is just silly. This can't be. What in the world is going on with me?"

I said, "No Lord, no, Lord, I was the little girl at Calvary Baptist Church; the preacher preached on hell. I went up front and shook hands with him..."

"You're *lost*."

I was shocked as much as anything because I thought I had done what I was supposed to do. I loved the Lord after my fashion and was involved in church work. I was not trying to fool anybody.

I could explain the plan of salvation; I knew how to lead somebody to Christ. I knew none of that saved you, but I still thought, "That can't be right."

And I thought, "Okay, this feelin' will go away when I get home. This is just Satan trying to deceive me. It'll be all right when I get home."

It wasn't all right. For the next two weeks, I wrestled with the conviction that I was a sinner. I couldn't talk to anyone, even Tim. Starting that night, I was quiet, and that's not my nature. Tim knew something was troubling me, but he didn't know what. How you see me, that's the real me, all the time; I'm little Miss Pollyanna; everything's great with the world. I'm sure he asked if anything was wrong, and I would say, "no." I couldn't talk about it to anybody!

I just couldn't tell a soul. I was too ashamed; I wanted to be wrong so badly because I thought, "How can I stand and tell people —they'll think I've been lyin' all this time?"

Like all people will tell you, when you're under conviction, you're sick, you're physically sick. It affects your appetite. I couldn't read a book and get rid of it; I couldn't watch TV and get out of it. I couldn't get any peace from anything because it was such an ominous burden. And so I wrestled, and I tried to talk God out of it.

I don't think I was trying to bargain with the Lord, but I was trying to convince myself, "Can this really be?"

It just became clear to me that I hadn't prayed the sinner's prayer. I thought, "Surely you prayed something; surely, surely!" I could remember the other things—going up, shaking hands with the preacher, and standing up on the communion table to shake hands with everybody. I guess that gripping fear I had dissipated; whatever I did must have made me feel better.

It became obvious to me that I had to agree with the Lord that yes, I'm in church, and I love church, and I love the Lord in my way—and I did—but the Lord was absolutely right about me. I was just going to have to do something, or I couldn't get any peace at all. So I grappled with this for two weeks.

One night, deep in the night, I got up out of bed. Tim was sound asleep, snoring, like he always did. It was about 2:00 in the morning on March 19, 1974. I went into the spare bedroom, got down by the spare bed, and I confessed my sin and repented.

I knew it was real because I saw myself the way God saw me. I saw myself as an absolute sinner. I was condemned, and I knew it. I asked Him to forgive me and save me. I got up from there with peace.

That spare bedroom became an altar that night. I got up from there with assurance of salvation, and I've never had a doubt since then.

I wrote about it when it happened in the front of the Scofield Bible Mama gave me in Christmas 1970, so I would never forget how I felt. I wrote: "Precious Lord, I thank You and praise You for extending mercy to me, till I confessed my sin to you and repented on my knees, and asked You to come into my heart and save me on this nineteenth day of March, 1974, in the beginning hours of the morning. How sweet to have the burden lifted, and all praise to the One who said, 'My burden is light.' To God be the glory forever!"

I went forward the next Sunday at church. Everybody was shocked!

My church had a really dynamic pastor at that time, and we were having a revival of church members getting saved! I was one, and my brother was another.

I was scripturally baptized the next Sunday night. Back then, we all had poofy, teased-up hair (and I still do), and the joke was, "What is she gonna do with that hair when she comes up out of that water?" Well, I brought a towel, wrapped it around all that hair, and took care of it at home!

Over the years, I learned that you really can't love the Lord as a lost person the way that you can after He saves you. But it can still take a long time, because you have to live life, see Him work, and learn to trust Him over the years. Of course, I love Him more now than I did then. The relationship is richer now; that's what sanctification is all about.

When I look back and realize the plan He had for my life, it was imperative that He get me right with Him. He had to do it in a dramatic way, and He did.

It's possible to think that you're okay when you're still lost.

What happened to me when I was seven years old was not valid. It's not that a child that young can't be saved; it can be real for children, but in my case, it wasn't.

I couldn't explain why I didn't get under conviction for playing with a rock-and-roll band on Saturday night, and playing for church on Sunday morning. I was young, I loved the music, and I didn't think that was wrong. But I didn't have the Holy Spirit to guide me, and I wasn't thinking about my testimony back then.

If I had passed away during that time, anyone who knew me and went to my funeral would have said, "We know we'll see Di again."

But they wouldn't have. I'd have been in that crowd that heard, "Depart from Me; I never knew you."

Many, many people have a similar testimony. There are unsaved people who show up for every church meeting, three times a week. So I have a heart for lost church members.

6

The very first song I ever wrote was called "He is Able." It sounded like something the Rambos would've done, 'cause I wanted to sing just like Dottie! Looking back at that song now, it's not half-bad. I think I should try to get it recorded!

My family started singing several of my songs, including "Behold the Lamb" and "Boundless Love." ("Boundless Love" was old when I sent it to the Cathedral Quartet; we had sung it for years all around this part of the country.)

The first time another group cut one of my songs was a defining moment in my life.

Through the late 1970s, we were singing lots of dates with the Songmasters. They were as good as anybody touring at the time. In fact, they were the most amazing group I ever heard who were not full-time. Joe Kelsey was their emcee and bass singer; he was amazingly dynamic, funny, and great in front of an audience. He was a shouter—he just brought worship with him in his pocket!

His wife Marcy played piano and had a huge alto voice. Dale Shipley, their lead singer, later sang with Perfect Heart. Today, you would know their soprano, Debbie Spraggs, as Debra Talley!

Nelson Parkerson signed the Songmasters to a contract with Calvary Records. (Calvary Records, based in California, was also the Hinsons' label at the time.)

One night, after a singing that included both of our groups, Joe Kelsey came up to me and said, "Dianne, we're fixin' to make a record, a national release, and we want to record 'Behold the Lamb.' We want to know if that's okay with you."

I just about swallowed my tongue!

It never occurred to me that anybody but my family would sing my songs. Until that point, I never would have asked anyone. But Joe asked me, and I think that was crucial; I know that was God's plan.

The first time I saw them sing the song in concert rocked my world. It was in a little Baptist church in the boot-heel of Missouri. Tim and I were sitting there together.

It got a reaction much like "We Shall See Jesus" later did with the Cathedrals. It was just a big song. Joe Kelsey, the bass singer, narrated the last verse. It built, and when they sang that last chorus, the Spirit of God just fell. It was a huge thing with everybody on their feet.

To hear your song being sung in an atmosphere that induced worship, to see the audience reaction, the people shouting —it's so surreal, it's hard to describe.

The song is about the crucifixion. I don't remember when I planned to sit down and write it, but it just told the story of the crucifixion in a way that got several groups to record it. The Hoppers, Jerry & the Singing Goffs, and the Dove Brothers later cut it, but the Songmasters had the definitive version.

When they performed it all around our area, it got an amazing reaction. The record doesn't capture that; nothing could. (In much the same way, no recording of "We Shall See Jesus" captures what Glen Payne did in person.)

Joe Kelsey died young with a brain tumor. I always thought that if he had lived, the Songmasters would have been one of the leading family groups in Southern Gospel.

Nelson Parkerson, who ran Calvary Records, also ran the Songs of Calvary publishing company (Ronny Hinson's publisher). He signed me to a three-year contract.

When I got my very first royalty check from him for "Behold the Lamb," I took it to work, and copied it on the copy machine before I cashed it! I cut it, and colored it with little colors. I have it in a frame today, on my wall with a lot of the other music things. It wasn't any big, fat, huge amount, but it was my first royalty check!

When Nelson signed me to the contract, I was ignorant of anything having to do with the music business. I thought that he was going to push my songs. (I had written quite a few songs at that time.) He didn't, so I just rode the three years out.

A few of my other songs from the 1970s have been cut. The Songmasters put a ballad called "A Glimpse of Calvary" on a later record; that was after Debbie Spraggs Talley had left them.

"Mama, See the Man" was a regional hit for the Hoppers in the 1980s. It featured Claude Hopper and got a lot of requests at that time.

When Roger Bennett left the Cathedrals in the mid-1980s to start his own record company, he made a record with the Lesters. They cut a song of mine that Roger loved, "By Then." It had an easy-rolling, Country Gospel beat.

There is another way some of them got used, though the world wouldn't know about it. Tim was the first person to hear any of those songs back when I first wrote them. We had a music ministry together; he had songs of mine he was well known for, but which never moved on to be used by anyone else. One he sang was a neat little Country Gospel song called "I Lost My Heart on Sunday Morning." It's about a guy who wandered into church just to hear the music and didn't expect the preaching to hit him so hard. Everybody loved it, but I don't know if it would go now or not. I should try to get it recorded!

Before I signed with an exclusive publisher in the late '90s, the Cathedrals published my songs on a song-by-song basis. From the late '90s through today, the publishers have those songs on file, but I'm the only one who has lyrics to some of the earlier ones.

I had a three-ring binder. When I first started, I would write all the lyrics down and put them in it. (Back then, I remembered all the tunes.)

One day, the binder came up missing. I couldn't find it anywhere. I thought I might have left it at the church we were attending. We turned the house upside down.

Finally, Tim came over with this look on his face. He said, "Do you remember that I used to keep a box of kindling down by the piano?"

I said, "Yes."

He said, "Do you think you could have ever just laid it down there, maybe? I think I may have tossed that box."

I was able to retrieve some of those lyrics from scraps of paper in the piano bench. But some were just gone.

I didn't cry as much as he did; it grieved him so badly.

It's always been my intention to go back and do something with the songs that survived. When I go back and flip through them, I still remember some of the tunes. I can look back and see that my lyric writing has improved, as anyone's would. But there are still some fresh ideas which haven't been done yet.

7

In late 1979, Methodist Hospital System of Memphis offered Tim the position of Director of Housekeeping. It was quite a step up for him.

I was just crushed because I never had thought about leaving Blytheville. It was home to me, and I never thought I'd move away. That's when I learned what it really meant to be married and to leave your people!

Blytheville was one of those towns where the young people grew up, graduated, and left. It was a neat little town in a lot of ways, but wages were low and the cost of living was high. It wasn't a place to stay and prosper.

At the end of 1979, Tim went on to Memphis to find us a place to live. I stayed about a month with my mother in her house, finishing out my notice on my job.

In January 1980, he found us a condo in the Raleigh area in north central Memphis.

I didn't think I would ever leave my home church in Blytheville; I was a charter member and had been playing piano ever since it had begun. But we found a little church down there that we really liked, Covington Pike Baptist Church. Wallace Pruitt was the pastor. I played piano, and Tim was a substitute choir leader. It was a precious place—what we needed at the time. We made a lot of nice friends there.

Sometimes song ideas come from nowhere.

I went to work as a transcriptionist for three gastroenterologists, transcribing all their dictation. They were in a big high-rise building across from Baptist Hospital in mid-town.

I had to park in a huge multi-level parking garage. You get on one level, and you wind to the next. You wind, you wind, and you wind, and you finally get down to the bottom and onto the street. One day, as I was winding through the levels, I started singing the line, "Jesus, I believe what You said about Heaven."

I thought, "Well, I like that little groove! I like that!"

The song just started coming quickly. I finished it up over the next day or so.

What's so odd now that I look back all the way to 1980, there was a line, "With all the news we're hearin' / our hearts have started fearin'." Somehow, even in 1980, that was on my mind. But that's tame to what we're fearing now!

Not too long after that, I went to work for the Veterans Affairs (VA) Hospital in Memphis. I had ten or eleven years of Civil Service in my background; when you leave Civil Service, you can pick it right back up with your seniority intact.

Every Thursday, the VA would have a real church service in the morning for patients and their families. Employees would come down to make a choir, and there was preaching.

One morning, they asked a Pentecostal girl who worked with me in medical transcription to sing. She had a voice like Vestal Goodman and could just sing up a storm! She asked me if I'd play piano for her, and I did.

Gail Davison (Gail Stidham at the time) was in the choir. I did not know her; I didn't really know anyone outside of my department; it was too big of a hospital. When the service was over, I noticed her coming down out of the choir, walking straight toward me. She said, "I wanna know your name, and I want to get to know you because I know we're going to be friends!"

I said, "Well, I'm Dianne Wilkinson, and why do you think that?"

Come to find out, she was born and raised in Mississippi, going to Baptist churches just like I did, and singing alto with her family at county singing conventions. She loved quartet singing, and even played piano for her church. We had so much in common.

The people we worked with didn't even know about this whole part of our world. It was almost like I was a closet Gospel singer and songwriter. But when I met Gail, I had a boon companion, who loved it like I did.

She watched my early songwriting career blossom; she was there at the very beginning. Before she got married in her late thirties and moved to Iowa, we would go to a lot of singings together. Tim went to some, but she would drive further. We would drive all night to Jackson, Mississippi for their annual Thanksgiving Eve singing—knowing we would have to drive all night to get home and get to our respective mothers' houses for Thanksgiving dinner, with no sleep!

Tim would say, "Y'all have a good time! I'll see you when you get back!"

But that's how eat up with it we were. She was a great companion to go to singings with, 'cause she didn't care how far away it was, she was game! She loved it like I did and still does! She is just the most precious friend. There's nobody like Gail.

Eddie Crook, pianist for the Happy Goodmans band, was my hero as a piano player. I knew he did session work in Nashville. So in 1981, I approached him and timidly asked, "How much would it cost for us to go into the studio and demo some of my songs?"

He told me that it would cost $1000, an incredible amount of money in 1981!

Since I didn't know any better, I asked him, "Do you think you could get the three other guys from the Goodman band to play?"

He said, "Sure!"

We worked hard to make arrangements for twelve songs. Tim and I had done a little singing with Gail, on a limited basis, around Memphis. So she joined us. She worked like a Turk on those songs; we'd put them on tape, and she'd take them home and learn her part, since I didn't have music written down to any of them.

I wrote "Turn Your Back" literally just a few days before we went to Nashville. I asked, "Have we got time to learn it and get it on there?"

Tim said, "We gotta put it on there; I think it's real strong."

So Gail knuckled down, bless her heart, and we learned it.

We recorded the demos in Nashville at the Oak Ridge Boys Studio. That was a big deal, even then. We went inside, and there was the band—Eddie Crook (pianist), Steve "Rabbit" Easter (utility musician), Bruce Droit (drummer), and James Gordon Freeze (bass guitarist)—ready to play.

The first song we did that day was "Boundless Love." When they played through it, I thought, "Oh, that's too fast, that's too fast!"

But it was Eddie Crook, for Heaven's sake! I was just in awe of him. He was a great guy, and he would've been glad to slow it down, but I just couldn't make myself speak!

Of course, if it was now, I'd have what it takes to say, "You know, I need you to slow that down about three clicks; that's what it needs." But I was too intimidated by my hero, Eddie, to say, "Hey, we gotta slow it down!"

He didn't think he was making a record; we were just doing a demo. He probably thought, "Well, surely she'd tell me." The rest were like I played them, so that's really the only one he got too fast.

When the Cathedrals recorded "Boundless Love" years later, they backed it right into the pocket, with my original tempo and groove. They got it just right.

At the time, I thought that "Jesus, I Believe What You Said About Heaven" was going to be my favorite. I liked the rock-flavored groove, and the band did a spectacular job on the demo. James Gordon Freeze was just wearing the bass out! It came out sounding like a real cut, instead of just a demo.

We had sung "Boundless Love" a long time, and I loved it, but it was new to Gail. She looked at me one day and said, prophetically, "That's the one that's going to do it for you, girl, right there. That's the one!" And it really turned out to be. My brother had always said that, too.

I've rarely been nervous as a performer, but I was really, really nervous that day. It was the Happy Goodman band, my songs were on the line, and Tim and I had borrowed the $1000. As it turns out, with "Boundless Love," "Turn Your Back," "Jesus, I Believe What You Said About Heaven," and "Mama, See the Man" on there, it was a good investment!

8

The Cathedral Quartet started in 1963, when Earl and Lily Fern left the Cathedral of Tomorrow in Akron, Ohio. Three of the Weatherfords' members at the time, Glen Payne, Bobby Clark, and Danny Koker, stayed with Rex Humbard and started the Cathedral Trio. The trio became a quartet when George Younce left the Blue Ridge Quartet to join them in 1964.

The Cathedrals worked up north almost exclusively during their early years; I don't remember seeing them in the '60s. I do remember seeing George with the Blue Ridge Quartet, before he joined the Cathedrals. And I was always impressed with Glen Payne's work with the Weatherfords.

I first remember seeing the Cathedral Quartet in the 1970s, after J.D. Sumner moved the National Quartet Convention to Nashville. The first lineup I remember had George Amon Webster and Roy Tremble with them. They were a great quartet, but they had not reached that special place yet. If I had known what was to come, I'd have paid more attention!

I took a lot of copies of the cassette from the Eddie Crook demo session to the 1981 National Quartet Convention. I passed them out to quite a few people. Actually, Eddie himself was interested in some of the songs at the time.

I put one in Kirk Talley's pocket. It was a momentous occasion.

He was singing tenor for the Cathedrals and screening songs for them. When I told him who I was, my name clicked with him, because he was with the Hoppers when "Behold the Lamb" was a regional hit for them. I still think that may be the only reason he listened; I know they don't listen to everybody who sticks a tape in their pockets! But he knew I wasn't a newbie, and that the tape probably deserved a listen.

Kirk's brother Roger was also with the Hoppers at the time. Roger wound up marrying Debbie, who sang soprano on the Song Masters record that introduced "Behold the Lamb." So the Talley brothers were well acquainted with the song! It opened the door to Kirk, and Kirk opened the door to the Cathedrals. That's the song the Lord used to start my songwriting journey.

By the time I got home from Convention, Kirk was already on the phone! I did have the good sense to put my contact information on the tape; I can't believe I knew to do that! He really liked several of them; I was overwhelmed.

When Kirk played that cassette for Glen and George, they put three on hold—"Turn Your Back," "Jesus, I Believe What You

Said About Heaven," and "Boundless Love." They really loved "Boundless Love," but it took five years for them to record it!

The first one they picked was "Turn Your Back," which was interesting because it was the last one written and almost didn't make it onto the cassette we made. I had just written it, and we really had to do some hot-footin', as Roger Bennett would say, to learn it in time for the demo session. That's the one they cut first.

I didn't think the Cathedrals would record "Jesus, I Believe What You Said About Heaven," because of that little rock beat! But Kirk talked them into it. It was my second cut with them, and I loved the way they did it! Kirk kept the groove right there.

The Cathedrals' version didn't do a whole lot. The record, *Favorites Old and New*, included a number of songs they'd cut before; it was like a table project.

But when Kirk founded the Talleys with his brother Roger and sister-in-law Debra, he talked Roger and Debra into doing it.

Then Kirk brought it back with The Trio! I saw The Trio (Anthony Burger, Ivan Parker, and Kirk) at the Frank Arnold Songfest in Jackson, Tennessee. Kirk came to me and said, "I got a surprise for you!"

I said "Yeah?"

He said, "We're going to sing 'Jesus, I Believe What You Said About Heaven.' Guess what else?"

"What?"

"We're gonna send it to the radio!"

I said, "Well, hey!"

It was the first time it went to radio. It didn't chart high, but it charted.

So I got three cuts on that song because of Kirk Talley. The cuts were all pretty true to his original arrangement; he liked the way he had done it!

After I heard that the Cathedrals were going to record "Turn Your Back," Gail and I went down to Alabama to see them in concert. (They hadn't cut it yet, but I knew they were going to.)

When Gail and I pulled up to the hotel, we could see their bus. I always get excited when I can see the bus. That day, I was so excited I thought I was going to faint!

We went to a restaurant to get something to eat. We didn't dream they were going to be sitting in there, but there they were! That's when Kirk introduced me to Glen Payne. Glen looked at me and started singing, "Who's that man with the cross on His shoulders" (the first few lines of "Behold the Lamb").

He said, "That is a great song that I have always wanted to sing."

I didn't dream he would have known that song. But Kirk had told him that this lady who wrote "Turn Your Back" had written it. That's my first memory of meeting Glen.

When I wrote "Turn Your Back," I was thinking about the whole idea of repentance. It's a turning thing. I thought of somebody who had a sad past in their lost life. When they get saved, they turn their back on the old life and choose to walk a different path.

Here's the funny thing: I didn't write it for George Younce. Unless it's a specific kind of song that I intend for the bass to shine on and lead, I don't write for the bass to take the lead. I write for the lead singer, and then at some point, I figure I'll mod it up high enough to where the tenor will take it to the treetops!

But when you're picking songs, quartet members share the features, so they picked it out for George. It turned out to be a great move. He was the perfect one!

The funniest story I have about the song was not from them. Just a couple of years ago, Gold City bass singer Aaron McCune found that song on YouTube. He's a big Cathedrals fan, of course, but he'd never heard it.

He went flying up to Daniel Riley—Gold City was looking for songs—and said, "I have found the greatest song by the Cathedrals! Must be old, they look young enough."

He played it for him, and Danny started grinning. He said, "You've never heard that?"

Aaron said, "No!"

"Then you don't know who wrote it."

"No!"

Danny said, "That's one of Dianne's! That's one of the first ones they ever cut of hers!"

Aaron said, "You're kidding!"

He said, "No!"

And so help me, two or three weeks later, Triumphant Quartet baritone Scotty Inman found the same song on YouTube. He hadn't ever heard it, either. He loved the song and got excited. (I love how the song transcends the decades, when young people still love the same songs young people in 1981 loved! That's just so cool!)

Scotty went flying up to his father, Clayton, to play it for him. Just like Daniel Riley, Clayton started smiling.

"Son, you don't know who wrote that, do you?"

"No!"

He said, "That's Dianne's first cut ever with the Cathedrals!"

Well, I'm Scotty's honorary grandmama, so he was really surprised!

Bottom line, Aaron and Gold City cut that song, and so did Triumphant, weeks apart. (Of course, Scotty is a baritone, so Eric Bennett actually sang the solo.) Both cuts were very true to the original; those bass-singin' boys didn't wanna change a thing! So I thought, "How my George would love that!" To know that two young guys, to whom he was a hero, discovered the song on YouTube and recorded it.

When the Cathedrals released *Something Special*, and I held the record in my hand, I was in shock. I couldn't believe that I had something by a major quartet. I thought, "That is your name! That is your name, and it's the Cathedral Quartet!" And Tim was even more excited; he was just beside himself.

Of course, I couldn't possibly know what was to come; I thought, "If this is the only cut I ever get, it's more than I ever thought would happen to me. How great is this?"

"Turn Your Back" was never sent to radio, but it actually got on the Singing News chart. The singles system wasn't as set in stone as it is now. It was a catchy little tune, and there were a lot of people playing it.

"Step Into the Water," written by Kirk Talley, was also on *Something Special*. It stayed #1 for seven months, when *nothing* stayed #1 that long. That's when I knew, "Yeah, that's a real good record to have a song on!"

No wonder "Turn Your Back" charted; it's like everybody wanted that record. It was just an amazing thing.

I put it this way: That's when I knew I had hitched my wagon to the right star! The Cathedrals were absolutely on the ascent right at the time I got hooked up with them. I put that cassette tape in Kirk's pocket when they were just about to explode and become the quartet of the age.

They were on the rise, and every record just took them further and made them more beloved. I had songs on all of those, so I made that journey with them.

In the process, I learned to love them like family, and love their families. The relationship was so sweet on a professional *and* personal basis, and this lasted until they retired in 1999.

Kirk Talley was a different sort of tenor—what I can only describe as "a tenor with soul." It was almost a Pentecostal kind of soul tenor, though he grew up Freewill Baptist! You wouldn't think that kind of soul tenor would fit with really traditional Glen and George, but it did. Kirk had those dimples and that million-dollar smile, and the crowd just loved him. I think he was a big part of them going up like they did in the early '80s.

Kirk and Mark Trammell were both young, but Mark has an old soul. He was old when he was young; even though he didn't look old, he was old on the inside, and that's a *good* thing!

Roger Bennett was the perfect person on the piano, and he was also funny. Add those three to Glen and George, and they had all the ingredients. It's like the Bible expression, "all things work together for good." So they just had it all going on.

Kirk, and later Roger, knew exactly how to screen songs and pick the right ones. They listened a lot to Bill Gaither and Lari Goss; those guys knew what to do and had great advice.

It just seemed like it built. Every record was a little more classy, and the Cathedrals' legend was growing.

Years earlier, when "Behold the Lamb" came out, my grandmother was afraid that the people handling the business side (not the Songmasters) wouldn't get me what I was supposed to get. She said, "That could happen so easy. How will you ever know if you're gettin' your part of the money you're supposed to get?"

When I really developed the relationship with the Cathedrals, I saw how they kept books and did business. Had she been alive, my darling grandmother would have been so proud of them. Every penny was accounted for, everything was honorable, and everything was right on the statement. It was all it should have been. She would have loved that.

9

I wrote "We Shall See Jesus" in early 1982. When I wrote it, I was thinking about the pivotal times in Jesus' ministry, when He was out on a hillside, where people gathered. I thought, "You know, that's where He gave the Beatitudes. That's where he performed the miracle with the little boy's lunch."

In the part of the country where they were, the people were out in the open a lot. They didn't have a great big First Baptist Church to meet in—so they often gathered together in great crowds on hillsides.

So many huge things happened in Jesus' life and ministry on a hillside. He healed people on a hillside. He preached to them. And, of course, He died on a hillside, and He ascended from one. He's going to come back, and touch His foot on that same one again!

I thought, "That's just a neat thought, all the times they were gathered on a hillside." So I built a trilogy of verses around the hillside idea—"once on a hillside."

Then I realized: When those people were on that hillside, they were looking at Him as though He was just like anybody else. He wasn't! He looked like most Jewish men did to the people. I thought, "I'm going to see Him just like they did, except I'm going to see Him glorified!"

I thought, "You know, they don't have anything on me! They saw Him, but one of these days, I'm going to see Him—as John says, 'it doth not yet appear ... [but] we shall see Him as He is.'"

Later, after I got more mature in my Bible study, I remember thinking that I'll see Him like John saw Him on Patmos. The glorified Christ was such a sight that poor John fell out like a dead man when he saw him!

I started a fourth verse, but later crossed it out. I don't remember what it was about; I didn't even keep a copy. Wherever I was going with it, I changed my mind. After I got rid of that verse, the song came pretty quickly.

At the time, I didn't know anything about the rules of professional songwriting, so I was just going on instinct as to how to structure songs. I just knew instinctively that we shouldn't do the chorus till the end. It couldn't say "We Shall See Jesus" until after all those experiences on the hillside; it had to build to that point.

Back in those days, Kirk Talley was singing "I Know a Man Who Can." I thought, "You know, this could be a new ballad for Kirk because it's got some range to it." So I sent it to him.

They passed on it. But because I didn't know any better, I sent it to him again! I wrote him back, and I said, "Are you sure? 'Cause I'm just sure this one's for y'all. Please listen to it again."

I didn't know you couldn't do that! Of course, we'd become friends by then, but how green was I? No writer does that. Had I been a seasoned one, I wouldn't have, either.

That's probably about the time when I thought, "Well, this is great! They didn't respond the first time, so you just send it back, and they'll see the light!" When you're first getting started, you don't know the norm; you're just doing what you think. And then you learn protocol for pitching songs.

Ever since then, I've never sent a song back and said, "I don't think you really listened to this one! I think you should listen again!" I've tried really hard not to be a pest.

All I know is that God was in it because then I was told, "Well, we're recording two of your songs, and we want you and Tim to come to Atlanta and be our guests for this live album." They told me that they were going to do "We Shall See Jesus" and "I'm Going Home Someday."

When Kirk had brought them this song, George looked at Glen and said, "Well, this looks like this is going to be a song the old man's going to be singing." (Only George would call Glen "the old man.") And they all said, "Yes, this is going to be Glen's song."

Tim's sister Jolene lived in Atlanta at the time with her family, so we had a built-in place to stay. (Tim was the oldest of three.) We went to her house and got ready for the concert. When we got to the auditorium, the Cobb County Civic Center in Marietta (an Atlanta suburb), it was bristling with excitement. They had our seats blocked off on the front row.

We were milling around in the lobby, and Bill Traylor walked over. He had just founded Riversong and signed the Cathedrals; he was there that night to produce the project.

He said, "Are you Dianne?

I said, "Yes."

And he said, "Dianne, you're not going to believe how Glen's going to sing your song."

I thought Bill was talking about "I'm Going Home Someday!" But I could tell from the way he was talking, he was talking about "We Shall See Jesus." I said, "No, Kirk's going to sing that one."

He said, "Oh, no, I've heard it, and Glen's going to sing it. You're just not going to believe how great it is. Wait till you hear Glen sing it."

I thought, "Glen? Okay." He was trying to prepare me!

When they sang it, I was just stunned by what I heard. Of course, the audience was on their feet through the whole chorus. But I thought—and the Cathedrals did, too—that it was because the crowd had been primed, "Go nuts, 'cause it's a live record!"

But we got to Quartet Convention that year, the same thing happened on the main stage. And an amazing thing happened when they did "We Shall See Jesus" in the Chapel service. The Lord just fell on that place. I'll never forget how it felt.

As I was making my way to the door, someone whom I did not know followed me out. It was Paul Heil; he already had *The Gospel Greats* going. He said, "I'd like to approach you about something I've never done before. I've never done a feature on one of my programs on a non-artist, but I'd like to do one on you." So I was the first.

The Cathedrals didn't change anything I had in mind about the trilogy of three verses. The only thing they changed, and I must give credit where credit is due: Kirk had the idea to put the second verse in the minor key. It wasn't my idea.

At the time, I thought, "That's just someone's arrangement of the song." Sometimes groups will do things like that when they do the arrangement. But it's become such a huge part of what made the song what it was.

The Cathedrals never encored that song—ever. With the crowd on their feet, still wanting more, it never happened. George just instinctively knew that it would be anticlimactic.

All the time, people ask me, "When are you going to write another 'We Shall See Jesus'?" But you can't just pull one of those out of the air. It's not like the Lord's going to drop one like that on you every two days! You couldn't handle it if you had a song that big every time you turned around. He knows what you can handle.

The amazing thing is, to this day, that's not my normal kind of song to write. I don't write big, fat ballads very often. I can, I have quite a few. But uptempo songs are my favorite to write.

I've had hopes for songs like "High and Lifted Up" or "Home Free" being the closest thing to a follow-up. But they haven't had the impact that one had. Except for "High and Lifted Up," they didn't have the Cathedrals, with all the charisma, nostalgia, and love for people that they had. It just all worked together.

I don't know if "We Shall See Jesus" would have been that huge a song with another group at that time. They were the right group and the right lead singer, at the right time, for the right song.

After the Cathedrals recorded "I'm Going Home Someday," Kirk pitched it to Gold City, and they recorded it on *Gold City: Live*. Back then, more than one group would do a song.

In my naïveté, here's what I was thinking. "This is really easy! It's a piece of cake! Falls off of my fountain pen, shows up on a record!" Well, I learned that not everything that goes out gets cut!

There is some romance and nostalgia attached to a piece of tablet paper with your handwritten scrawling on it, of a song which became iconic. That's just an amazing thing. I have always saved those scratched-up sheets.

I had the tablet paper for "We Shall See Jesus," scratched-out fourth verse and all. (I thought I had tossed the fourth verse.) I left it just like that—regular lined, white legal-pad paper, with a ballpoint pen. The beauty of it is, you want it to be just like you got it, scratch-outs and all.

Glen Payne celebrated his fiftieth year in Gospel Music in 1994. I was invited to a special event in a ballroom of a hotel in downtown Nashville. It had to be a big ballroom, because his wife, Van, had bought him a gorgeous, brand-new pickup truck, and they drove it in there where he could see it! How they got it in, I didn't know!

I didn't tell any of the guys that I was going to do this, but I took the original lyrics to "We Shall See Jesus" to a frame shop, and had it framed.

I had wrapped it in brown paper, so nobody could possibly have known what it was. I propped it up against one of the chairs, so nobody noticed it.

All kinds of dignitaries were there. There was a program; obviously, they had put some time into who was going to speak. His children got up and spoke. I didn't want to break in unannounced.

Right toward the end, I went up to Roger and said, "Roger, I have somethin' with me that I want Glen to have, but I didn't wanna break into the program. But I'd like to present it to him while people can see it, because it's really special."

He said, "What is it?"

I answered, "It's my original lyric sheet to 'We Shall see Jesus.' I had it framed for him."

Roger's face just went white. He said, "You go get it, hold on, hold on," and went to get Glen.

It was basically over, but people were still visiting at the tables. Someone, probably Roger, said, "Wait just a minute, folks, we have something special we didn't know we were going to get."

I told Glen that I had something for him, and when he looked at it, he would know what it was.

One of his favorite words was "wow." I think that was the first thing he said when he saw it, and, of course, he teared up.

I said, "It's my original tablet paper that I wrote 'We Shall See Jesus' on, scratch-outs and all. Glen, it means everything to me to give you this."

It was a special moment, just a sweet, sweet thing. By 1994, he and I both knew what the song had been and was.

The last time I ever saw Glen was at the Cathedrals' Farewell concert at the Ryman. He sang "We Shall See Jesus" there. Then I sat at his funeral, and watched him sing it on video. Glen and I came full circle with "We Shall See Jesus"—it took two decades.

I can't believe it has been thirty years. It just doesn't seem possible!

10

Tim and I decided that even though he still worked at Methodist Hospital in Memphis, it would be better to live in West Memphis, which was right across the Mississippi River in Arkansas. Memphis was so big that it was a commute for us anyway, and big cities have more crime. So we bought a house in West Memphis and fixed it up.

West Memphis was a smaller town, more like Blytheville. All you have to do is drive across the Mississippi River Bridge to go shopping; you can have the best of both worlds. Plus, my mother's brothers, Uncle Raymond and Uncle Marvin, lived there. That was a big deal for me, because I'm very close to my family. I could see both of their houses on the way to work; I felt so wonderfully secure!

When we moved to West Memphis, I went to work at the local hospital, Crittenden Hospital. Mrs. Lois Cain, the Director of Medical Records, made me her assistant. She was a precious little lady, and she let me do all my favorite things, like coding and medical staff committee work. I was very happy there.

Because of the work I do, I'm heavily involved with the medical staff wherever I work. The medical staff there was one of my favorites. I thought some day Mrs. Cain would retire, and I would become the director. I guess I could have stayed there forever.

We visited several churches, but just had not found the one we were looking for. We weren't looking for the big First Baptist Church; we liked the smaller churches. One day, a friend from work, Michael Etheridge, said, "I know where you need to be goin' to church, but you'd have to drive about thirty minutes to get there. There's a little town called Forrest City, Arkansas, and it's on down farther from West Memphis toward Little Rock."

He said, "The best man I ever knew, Brother Dan Minton, is pastor of the Second Baptist Church down there. You'll love him and his wife Shirley. You'll love that church, and they'll love y'all, and they need y'all to help with their music. You just drive down there and see."

Well, we did, and everything he said was true! We fell in love with that church. They put Tim in as choir leader, and I played piano. Brother Dan was the most precious, twinkly-eyed, darlin' fellow, and he just loved music.

Because Tim was not a Blytheville native (he was an Okie who relocated to Arkansas), he was just known as my husband. But in Forrest City, nobody knew either one of us, and it became more Tim and Dianne, more like a real couple. He came into his own and blossomed down there.

They loved for him to sing my songs, or for us to sing them together. Brother Dan loved the country-flavored ones; I would tease him—it was such an informal church—he'd say, "I know, I know you're going to say I've been listenin' to country radio again! I know you're going to say I love George Jones!"

I'd say, "Well, you do!"

And he said, "I do, I do, I'm guilty!" He had so much wit about him. He was a very loving man, and his wife was precious. They loved us, and we loved them.

The first people who ever heard any of the songs I wrote back then, like "Innocent Blood" (Hoppers) or "Gospel Music on My Radio" (Dean Hopper), were those people at Second Baptist. Tim would sing them first, and he could just wear 'em out!

The other thing was, those folks really dug down into their pocketbooks and gave, and some of the biggest Southern Gospel groups at the time came to that church.

So here I was in West Memphis, in a pretty house, near my uncles, in a job I loved, and so happy in that church—and so help me, in 1985, Tim came to me and told me he wanted to move!

I thought, "You want to do *what*?" I just couldn't believe my ears.

He got an offer to be Director of Housekeeping at the hospital in Jackson, Tennessee. It's now the flagship of West Tennessee Healthcare, the biggest hospital between Memphis and

Nashville, and one of the ten biggest health care systems in the country.

He wasn't liking how things were going at Methodist. He wanted out of the whole Memphis midtown thing, and it was a better deal for him career-wise.

I have to admit, I cried while I was packing, and I cried while the people were coming to load the truck. He knew how unhappy I was about it, but he figured I'd get over it. I guess you get over everything. But I don't know when I had ever been so blue about moving away.

Plus, we were going back to a big hospital, and I didn't like big hospitals any better than I did big churches. Earlier that year, I had fallen on the ice and torn all the ligaments in my right knee. I was still on a cane, and I wasn't going to be able to get around the campus of that hospital very well.

We found a small place in Jackson. He wanted to build a house, so we found a little house to live in until then.

I still have a picture of the last Sunday we were at Second Baptist. Someone took a picture of the Mintons and us; the Mintons looked like they were at a funeral. I know Brother Dan thought he was losing a lot when we left. It was hard for me to leave that sweet church.

In about 1986, Tim got a call from Randy Hoover with Methodist Hospital. Methodist Hospital is a system, with hospitals all around this area; at the time, they owned the one in Dyersburg.

Randy, who knew Tim's talents, said, "I want you to come to work as one of my system administrators. We wanna renovate this building, and I want you to head that up."

Our plan was to continue to live in Jackson; Tim would commute to Dysersburg. Dyersburg is a small town, about the same size as Blytheville and West Memphis; inside, I wished I could go to the little town and small hospital, too!

In 1987, their Director of Medical Records quit. Randy called me to come up and interview; he said: "I think you need to be Director of Medical Records down here, and then you and Tim could just move." I was so happy that I could've fallen down on the ground like the Jews do when they get to the Wailing Wall!

I had made some friends in Jackson, and I loved going there to shop and do things, but it was way bigger than I would ever want to live in. Also, we never found a church there; they were all too big!

So we moved to Dyersburg, into a little subdivision called Rolling Meadows. Dyersburg felt like the perfect fit the way West Memphis did (and the way Jackson and Memphis didn't!) We eventually built a house out from town in the Lakewood area, on a man-made lake.

The first church we visited was Hawthorne Baptist Church. It was in our neighborhood. We fell in love with that little church, the preacher, and everything about it.

One day, we got a call from the folks at Springhill Baptist Church. They had gone to a singing where I had been introduced as a songwriter. They wanted to know what it would take to get us to come out there and help with the music. We said we'd come and see.

As we walked in, a marvelous white-haired bass singer was leading "When the Saints go Marching In." We thought, "Well, we're going to like this!"

The church dated back to the late 1800s, but it had gotten to be quite small; there were maybe fifty people in Sunday School. We just fell in love with the older people out there; Tim and I always loved older church people. We loved their wisdom and just loved to be around them. It never bothered us if we were the only younger ones on a church trip.

They wanted Tim to direct the choir, and they wanted me to play piano, so we began doing that.

Brother Don Laymon was preaching at the time; he was an interim pastor. One day, one of the gals from the pulpit committee came up to me. She said, "We've heard about this young man from over in Paragould, Arkansas, and we just wondered, do you know him—his name's James Branscum."

I said, "Yes, I do—he's my brother!"

Maybe some of the others on the pulpit committee knew he was my brother. But I don't believe she knew, or she wouldn't have asked. That was the first time I realized they were interested in Jim.

Jim didn't know at the time that this was my church, or he would've called me.

God moved in the situation because it had been a dream of ours to work in a church together. Tim and Jim were as close as blood brothers.

Jim hadn't been in the pastorate very long; he's four years younger than I am. The pulpit committee had heard about him, and went out to Paragould, Arkansas, to hear him.

Well, he was a fireball back then, and they really liked him. They brought him over in view of the call, and Jim said, "Now let me get this straight; y'all would have me preachin', and my sister on the piano, and my brother-in-law leadin' the singin', and it would be okay with y'all?"

They said that they didn't care how many of our family were there—they thought that would be great!

The church just grew and grew, and God blessed it. The singing was tops. Jim can sing the stars right out of the sky, and we could put groups together from among our family. He had a radio program, and his little Rachel, my niece, was singing on the radio before she was old enough for kindergarten. She could harmonize with a buzz-saw! And we had other people in the church who could sing.

When you're a singing church, the word really gets out. When quartets were coming through, they'd call, so we started having singings there.

I was asked to teach the Open Door Sunday School Class after someone left. I'm still teaching that class!

That little church just took off!

11

After Kirk Talley left the Cathedrals to start the Talleys with his brother Roger and sister-in-law Debra, Roger Bennett took over screening songs for the Cathedrals. Kirk just had a sense of what would work for the Cathedrals; Roger did, too, so he made a perfect follow-up.

I don't know if I've ever had a relationship just like the one I had with Roger Bennett. He was like a son to me—the funniest kid I ever knew. I watched him grow up. I loved his family. We were so close, he was like the other side of my soul—he knew what I was going to say before I ever said it!

I couldn't be called anything but a new writer in every sense of the word. Here were the Cathedrals, on the ascendant. What are the chances of a gal from Blytheville that had had one cut in her life getting on that train and riding it all the way to the end of the depot?

Roger kept my songs before Glen and George. Other than the Eddie Crook demo, I never had a professional demo to send them. I sat at my piano, a Baldwin Acrosonic, with my boombox and cheap tapes, and played and sang the songs. We were living from check to check, and I didn't even buy good tapes!

I'd set the lyrics in front of me; sometimes they were handwritten, and sometimes I typed them at work on my IBM Selectric II typewriter.

I sang them myself; there were no harmonies. It helped that I was a strong pianist, and could get the chords I wanted. But I could play it better than I could sing high notes. If you talk to my quartet boys, they'll always tell you that when Dianne's trying to sing a quartet song, the range is awful! There are places where I'm going to have to literally holler or squeal to reach the note I want. But they understand it's what I have to do to show them what I want them to do. They're not looking for a quality vocal out of me when it's just a work tape.

I would send them to Roger; he could make Glen and George hear what was in those songs. That's how they heard "We Shall See Jesus," "All in God's Own Time," and "Goin' in Style."

One time, Roger said, with a twinkle in his voice, "Dianne, I don't say anything about your bongin' clock in that room where your piano is. I don't say anything about the cheap old tapes that you send me! I don't even talk about the little bell on the collar of your dog comin' through; I'm hearing that. I don't ever say anything about any of that. But you're going to have to tune your piano!"

I said, "What do you want, man? You don't want me to spend any money!"

How we laughed!

Everybody invested money in demos, but I didn't have any to invest!

Eventually, I got a Yamaha electric keyboard. They're in perpetual tune, so I don't have to worry about it. It's a good keyboard, but I have never liked playing on it as much, because I don't like the touch as much as a real piano's touch.

Toward the end of the Cathedrals' run, people were getting more sophisticated with what they were sending them. It was probably reaching the time where Glen and George weren't still going to be able to hear what I wanted them to hear from those work tapes. They listened, because they knew my track record. But we were probably getting right to the time when I was going to have to find a way to keep up with the other people who were sending them songs.

My fifth Cathedrals cut was "All in God's Own Time," on *The Prestigious Cathedral Quartet* album. One day, as they were getting ready to record with Lari Goss in Nashville, Roger called and said, "I'm callin' to invite you to come over; the guys want you to come over to the studio and hear them record your song."

I was so excited! I managed to get off from work and met them at a Shoney's, close to Music Row. I either followed the bus over, or Roger drove my car over, so we would get to the studio at the same time.

Lari Goss was there with them. The whole atmosphere was an easy atmosphere; they were having fun. It wasn't stressful, like

"We're never going to get this." (If the producer was really tough, you could really get some stress going!)

When they were cutting vocals for "All in God's Own Time," someone had the idea for George to talk through his part. It was a great idea.

I still remember when they did that jazzy high ending with the sixth in there—it was such a bright sound, and Danny Funderburk just nailed it in that high range. I thought, "Somebody just shoot me right now! I could just die right now! It could never get better than this; everything's going to be downhill from now on!"

I had promised Roger I could be quiet and not offer any instructions. (Even back then, I was giving instructions on the little tapes I sent in!) Since they were working on vocals, Roger was sitting with me. He said, "Well, I don't know if you can or not, but I'll be sitting close by, and I can restrain you if I have to!" As gracious as Lari Goss was, I'm sure he would not have thought he needed any advice from the songwriter! But as it turned out, I did not have to offer any advice, because it was absolute perfection.

I got to hear them working on "Build an Ark," as well.

I'm not sure if we broke for lunch or quit for the day, but they had some time off in the afternoon. Somewhere about mid-day, Roger said, "Guess where we're goin' this afternoon?"

"Where?"

"We're goin' over to Ben Speer's studio with Mark Trammell, and we're going to make a demo of 'Master Builder.'"

I had already sent the song to Roger. Our thought was, "We'll have to demo it and send it to the Nelons, because Glen and George ain't *ever* gonna do one with a rock beat! They're just not!"

It was more fun than I thought I would ever get to have in my life. When we got in there, Roger had only played it a few times, but I could play it full-out. Ben wanted me to play it so Roger could chart it. I was really wearing it out, playing rock-and-roll style. Ben didn't know me, but I never will forget when he came over and said, "You need to let her play it; I love that, I just love that." It just made me so happy!

Mark sang the demo solo. I thought, "Boy, what a shame they never will do that, 'cause Mark was *born* to sing that song." He was really putting his heart into it. We got a great demo.

When we finished, Roger, Mark, and I were all talking. Roger said, "My soul! Mark's the one that's supposed to sing this song!"

All three of us agreed, "Well, that's never going to happen, 'cause we'll never talk Glen and George into doing one with a rock-and-roll beat!"

Roger called me one night and said, "You're not going to believe what's happened!"

"What's happened?"

"The Cathedrals are going to record 'Master Builder.'"

I said, "Nooo ... this is one of your jokes." (By then, he was legendary for that kind of joke playing.)

He said, "No! Bill Gaither is producing our record. I don't even know what made me haul it out, but he heard Mark's demo of 'Master Builder.' He fell in love with it, and he talked Glen and George into doing it. It's going to be the title cut of the record!" So I have Bill Gaither to thank for that cut.

It was my first big-orchestrated, full-brass treatment of a song, especially one that was upbeat. When Roger sent me a rough cut, he said, "This is the one you've been waitin' for, Di; this is the big orchestration, big treatment. You've got to hear this."

When I heard it with all that brass, I'm telling you, I couldn't stand it—it was so good. Mark just *owned* it, and then Danny came in with "Jesus is the Master Builder"! Everyone repeats the chorus once, but they did three choruses at the end. It was like it was just too good to quit after one repeat, so they did it one more time!

I still love to write with that rock flavor, with songs like "The Rock's Between the Hard Place and You," and "He Picks Up a Beggar on the Way." "Master Builder" may have been the first of that type of rock-flavored quartet song to make it big.

It turned out to be so much of a signature song for Mark, that he has recorded it with every group he's been with since, except Gold City. It was great every time!

The Cathedrals cut three of my songs on *Travelin' Live*: "Homeland," "Boundless Love," and "I'm in the Shadow."

Roger hadn't done much singing before he sang "Homeland" on *Travelin' Live*. The song always makes me think of him; it was his favorite of mine for years. He told me once that after his mother died, he couldn't sing it for at least a year because it made him think of her so much.

Here's the best part of the story: It always had a second verse. I don't know why the Cathedrals didn't use it, except that they just kept wanting to go back and do that chorus again! So they decided to leave it off.

But Roger never forgot the second verse. When the Booth Brothers were going to cut it on their 2004 *Pure Southern Gospel* project, almost twenty years later, they called Roger. They wanted two verses, and they were just hoping there was a second verse that the Cathedrals had decided not to do. As long as it had been since I wrote it, Roger sang that second verse to them on the telephone without even going and looking up the words!

The Booth Brothers said, "Oh, we might even like it better than the first verse! We can't wait to do it!" When they did it, that's when everybody knew it had a second verse!

I had sent "I'm in the Shadow" to the Cathedrals along with a bunch of other songs. In pitching sessions, sometimes a member of the group will say, "You know, that's the one I want, right there. I want to do that one if nobody else does." As I recall, when they were listening to songs, Glen liked that one right away and said it was the one he wanted to do.

I was somewhat surprised about that, because all my career, I have never thought about the slow songs as the ones that would do much for me. But people still remember that song and love the way Glen did it.

Roger had always loved a song I wrote called "By Then." It's country-flavored and has a rolling ballad beat. It talks about the Tribulation, and where we'll be and what we'll be doing by then.

Roger left the Cathedrals from 1986 through 1988, working with the Eagle One record company. The Lesters cut that song on an album Roger produced. It's not a spectacular song, but it was one of Roger's favorites. To the day he died, Roger could still sing songs I had submitted that nobody had recorded; he never forgot them.

Mark Trammell screened songs for the Cathedrals until Roger returned. "Goin' in Style" was the only cut I got during that time, and it was another title cut.

Through the '80s, I got an occasional cut with somebody else. But mostly, my eggs were in that one big basket. I just didn't have the time or the wherewithal to get into songwriting in a big way; my healthcare career has always been a demanding one.

I got a few Hoppers cuts through the '70s and '80s. (They had already cut "Behold the Lamb" and "Mama, See the Man.") They cut "Innocent Blood," which is very doctrinal; they like that kind of song. Dean Hopper also cut two of mine, "Gospel Music on My Radio" and "On Crucifixion Day," on a solo record.

I would always tease Connie Hopper what an anomaly it was that any group with a woman was going to sing my songs. I could already tell that I was going to be a quartet girl all the way, 'cause that's where my heart was.

Through those years, I honestly thought that every song the Cathedrals cut would be the last one. No one was supposed to get sixteen cuts with them in two decades. That just didn't happen.

Nobody else had that kind of track record with them. And I was the new kid! So every time I got a song recorded, I thought, "Well, it's been a great run, you know?" Then I'd send 'em some more, and it just kept happenin'.

One year at the National Quartet Convention, I left early to get back home to get ready for work. When I left, the Cathedrals had just done "Boundless Love" and "We Shall See Jesus" back to back. Everybody in that place was on their feet. It was still kind of new to me, and I remember thinking, "Lord, I can't even believe it —I have no words!"

To this day, I still don't have words! When the Kingdom Heirs are closing out their set with "What We Needed," and the lights are swirling and the people are on their feet, there's no way in the world you can describe what that feels like. It has nothing to do with pride, vanity, or ego. It is just the most humbling thing. You're just sitting there thinking, "Lord, I'm just unworthy. How did I get to be this blessed person; how did that happen?"

12

In early 1989, Tim was diagnosed with cancer.

That same year, Methodist Hospital in Memphis offered us both jobs. Tim had worked there before, but I never had. They were opening a big new quality management department; they wanted me to be its centerpiece, for quality assurance activities, accreditation, and medical staff review processes. That was my forté back then, so it was quite a promotion.

When we made the move, Tim was already sick, so I worked out the sale of our house and found a place in Memphis. (The process started in '89, but it was probably '90 when we actually made the move.) At this point, I had a feeling that Tim wasn't going to get well, and I think he thought so, too. We thought the move would be the best thing because it was now my career that would need to be protected.

When we moved to Memphis, I grieved because we were so happy in Dyersburg, and we loved Springhill so much. But I knew we had to go where we could make the best living.

Tim had been baptized as a teenager and loved both church and gospel singing. But he wasn't really saved until after he got sick. One Sunday morning, when we were still in Dyersburg, I walked into the bedroom and found him sitting on the end of the bed, crying!

I said, "What's the matter with you?"

He said, "Well, I'm ashamed to tell you in one way, but I just asked the Lord to save me, and He just did."

So he went forward that day and made it public.

Tim's cancer progressed quickly. His mother, Mildred, was a widow then; she lived in Oklahoma. When Tim got really bad, she moved in with us and stayed through the end. It was such a blessing for me as I had always enjoyed his family like he had mine. What she did was a Godsend because I don't think I could have managed without her.

As they often do, they treated Tim really aggressively with both radiation and chemotherapy. He was in and out of the hospital. It was all just too much; by Christmas of 1990, his liver had begun to fail.

I still remember when we had him in the hospital, and they were giving him platelets. His doctor came in, and Tim said, "You know what, Doc, I'm not comin' back to get platelets again, I'm not comin' back to the hospital to do anything again. I'm goin' home, and I'm going to trust God."

When we got home from that hospital stay, we talked about it. It was a very freeing thing just to be able to talk about it: "Honey, I'm not going to get well, and you know that."

"Yes, I know that."

You can almost breathe out again and start living with the reality. So we got home health nurses in, and later hospice. We made all the funeral arrangements. He asked me to wear an outfit that he loved, a fuchsia and purple knit dress with a jacket. He picked out the songs and asked my brother Jim to preach and do the singing.

He talked about it like he was going to move again to another town, just changing locations.

On Friday, February 1, 1991, when I got home late in the afternoon, Mildred told me the nurses had said that this would be the day. Tim had been comatose for most of that week, and he was in what is called agonal breathing. The nurses said he wouldn't make it past night.

He began to breathe the death rattle. If you've ever heard it, you never forget it. Jim was by his bed, near Tim's knees. Mildred was beside Jim, closer to Tim's chest. And I was up close to his head. We were just standing around the bed because we just knew that one of those breaths would be the last.

He took one of those breaths. Then, for just an instant, he opened both his eyes, wide. The only way I can describe his expression was complete awe and wonder. It's almost like, if he could have spoken, he would have said, "You can't believe what I am seeing!" That's what his look said.

We saw him go over.

He shut them again, on his own; no one had to shut his eyes. He was forty-three years old.

When Jim left to go home, he looked at me and said, "Did you see what I saw, or do I just think I saw what I saw?"

I said, "If you're talkin' about seein' Tim go to Heaven, yes, we saw it!"

He said, "Well, it was the most amazing thing I ever saw."

We had already made arrangements with the funeral home in Blytheville. An ambulance came to Memphis from Blytheville to pick up his body.

When we left the room, nobody said all that much. Mildred and I didn't cry right then. Tim had suffered; when your liver fails, you can't eat, you can't taste food. It's a terrible way to die. Especially since we literally saw him enter the gates, it was like we not only couldn't cry, we were almost envious.

After Jim went back to Dyersburg, Mildred and I sat on the couch. She said, "Okay, what are we going to do? Are we going to go to bed, or are we going to get in there and clean out that room?"

Well, I knew what she wanted me to say. And I said, "We're going to get in there and clean up that room."

We set all the trappings of the sick room outside in the storage space so there would be nothing in that room to remind us that it was the sickroom. It was going to be Tim's room, but it wasn't going to be the sick room.

The funeral home in Blytheville was packed. I remember going through the motions, but it was like I was in a dream. Later on, when I looked at the registry, there were people who had come whom I didn't know were there.

Tim had requested that Jim sing his favorite hymn, "Where We'll Never Grow Old," and he did. Tim had recorded the Ronny Hinson song "First Day in Heaven" when we were with the Revelations, and I think we played that song so they could hear Tim sing it.

Mildred went home, and I went back to work. Methodist Hospital had brought me down to prepare for an accreditation commission. It was coming, so I had a lot to do, and it was good that I did. Through the whole thing, my way to deal with the sadness and grief had been to set it over in a corner, like a trunk. I thought, "I can't deal with you right now; I'll deal with you later." But eventually, it all hit.

That year, 1991, was the only year that I can remember not going to the National Quartet Convention. Of course, it wasn't on my mind.

After that, I got to the place where I thought, "I've got to get back in touch with the music and the music people because I need it." I didn't really know many people there in Memphis.

I saw in one of the Gospel Music papers that the Cathedrals, and quite a few other groups I loved, were going to be singing in St. Louis. Tim had left me some life insurance, and I wasn't in debt, so I was able to get a plane ticket and hotel room.

I didn't tell anyone that I was coming. I walked into the venue in St. Louis, and there they were—Roger, George, and Glen! Seeing them, and being with them, was more healing for me than medicine would have been. I had an IV infusion of singing that night! It was just a balm for my soul.

Of course Roger and the other guys had known Tim so well, and they had grieved about his passing. In fact, for years afterwards, Roger associated "Homeland" with Tim's passing.

God knew the end from the beginning. He brought Tim and me together as friends when I was engaged to his roommate! He knew, in His foreknowledge, when we would both be saved.

Tim was always loving to me; he was never mad. The only thing he ever did that I could have just pinched him for was all those moves—and now that I look back, it was God's plan all the way through. God used every one of them.

He was dynamite in job interviews. All he had to do was show up; employers would take him in a heartbeat! When he got bored, he never had to worry about a place to go!

He was good at what he did! In fact, the street in front of where I work now is called Wilkinson Drive, and it's not me, it's him! He designed the doctors' office buildings on that street after he got sick, and they named it in his honor.

I was so blessed in our marriage. In a marriage, if the wife gains some kind of fame, even if it's not worldwide, I think there's the potential for the husband to get to feeling like Prince Philip. My Tim was never like that! He *loved* it all!

He got to hear all the songs first. When I lost him, one of the hard things was, I thought, "I won't have a soundin' board anymore!"

But of course, he was always biased, he liked them all! If you didn't think I was the best songwriter in the world, you didn't *dare* tell him!

13

When Tim was sick, I just wasn't minded to write. The song that broke the long dry spell was "He is Mine."

In 1990, Mark Trammell left the Cathedrals to co-found Greater Vision with Gerald Wolfe. At the time, Greater Vision had an annual homecoming outdoors, on a mountaintop outside of Sevierville, Tennessee. I went in 1992 and took a cassette tape of "He is Mine" to slip into Mark Trammell's pocket. I couldn't hear anybody but Mark singing it.

I didn't know when they were going to record. I didn't hear anything from him for a long time. One day, he called, and I heard that slow Arkansas voice say, "Well, Di, I hope that song's still available, 'cause we recorded it today."

I said, "Well, I'm sure glad, 'cause you were who I wanted. Please tell me you got the lead, because you're supposed to have the feature!"

He said yes.

It's been one of the most enduring and most recorded songs I've had that wasn't a huge ballad or a big ole quartet song. People are still singing that song. In fact, of all the songs I've written, it's the only one that I know is in a hymnal.

My first Cathedrals cut in the '90s was "There is a Haven." I wrote it several years earlier, before Tim passed away. We were driving from Dyersburg across the Mississippi River to go to a funeral of a sweet, dear lady from our home church in Blytheville.

The song started coming to me in the car. I remember not having anything to write on; I tore a check out of my billfold and wrote it on the back of a check.

Tim could see what I was doing. By the time we got to Blytheville, I had that song finished.

It's very vanilla. So when I got ready to send songs for the next record, I almost didn't send that one. I thought, "I don't see anything spectacular about this one! It's not jivin' like 'Master Builder.' It doesn't soar to the treetops like 'We Shall See Jesus.' I'm just—well, who knows, send it on!" I sent five or six songs and thought it had the least chance of getting recorded.

When they had picked songs, Roger called and said, "Guess which one we're doing."

I said, "I don't know." I thought it was going to be one of the fast ones.

He said, "'There is a Haven.' George is crazy about it. It's his favorite you've ever done so far."

"Get out!" I said. "It's just so simple I almost didn't send it!"

"Don't ever do that!" Roger replied. "Send me *everything*, and let me be the judge!"

George just sang it so sweet; he had a verse, and Scott had a verse. It was the first record after Scott Fowler joined, so it was the first thing they recorded that featured him.

Through the years, I got so many comments about that song. As it turned out, people did like to have it sung at funerals. One time, a young man told me that he had sung it with his mother all around where they were located, and it was everyone's favorite song that they sang. When his mother passed away, he put "There is a Haven" on her tombstone.

You never know if a simple song without a huge groove, a huge bunch of key changes, and a whole lot of range will be the favorite. And to think I almost didn't send it!

It turned out to be the only song I got on that record. And till he died, it was George Younce's favorite one of mine. That's when I learned the lesson that you never know what's going to touch people.

When the Cathedrals were looking for songs for their next studio project, I sent them "High and Lifted Up." We didn't want anything to *replace* "We Shall See Jesus," but we thought it had the potential to be another for Glen to sing that was very like that one. It was strong for them, but nothing ever came up to that original one! It became a big choral hit, and many people still call it their favorite Cathedrals song.

I had to rework the first line of the chorus. I had started the melody low, then going up. They loved it, but it's hard to harmonize. Roger asked me if I would find something more singable, just for that first line. Of course, that was easy to do, and it turned out to be better that way.

I'll never know why Roger called me at work one day. They were actually in the studio, cutting the album. He told me how it was going and said, off-handed, "You don't have anything new that I haven't heard, do you?"

I said, "Well, I really do, because Saturday night Kirk was singing at a church in Memphis, and I drove down there and heard him. On the way home, I wrote one that's brand new, but it doesn't sound anything at all like y'all, 'cause I hear it kind of bluegrass."

He said, "Really?"

"Yeah. The name of it is 'Jesus Has Risen.'"

"Well, sing me some of it!"

Well, I did. And he just had a fit! "Gone / Gone"—and I really put the grass thing on it.

He said, "I love it!"

And I said, "YOU DON'T!"

He said, "I do. I'm going to chart it, and I'm going to play it for those guys tomorrow."

He called me the next day, and he said, "We cut that song, and Lari [Goss] has put hammered dulcimer on it. This song is not like anything we've ever recorded. It's way out of the box for us."

I said, "Well, I reckon!" 'Cause I was still hearing grass. You know, it would still work as grass.

They sent "Jesus Has Risen" to radio. It got to #2. I heard people say that what probably put it over was when Ernie Haase and Roger Bennett started doing dueling tenors on that song live. I think that really caught people's attention.

In 1995, it was nominated as one of the top ten songs for the Singing News Fan Awards. I had only been at my job a couple of months when it was time for Quartet Convention. I really wasn't even going to try to ask off and go because I didn't think it had a chance of winning. I thought that the big Kingsmen hit, "I Will Rise Up From My Grave," by Jack Toney, was a shoo-in.

Even as popular as the Cathedrals were, I thought there was no way the song would win. But then I got to thinking, just on the off chance, perhaps I should go. I didn't have tickets, I didn't think I could find a room. My boss said, "Absolutely, take a couple days and go." Back then, awards were on Thursday night, so I went on that night.

I had gained some weight, and I didn't really have the kind of dress I would have wanted to win in. I didn't think I had a chance anyway, so I just brought a dress like I'd wear to church.

Back then, they didn't seat any of the songwriters who wrote nominated songs in the artist circle, unless they just happened to be in the group. I bought a ticket the night I got there, and boy, was I up in the cheap seats!

The ten nominated songs were performed. When the last one was being sung, I thought, "What am I going to do? I can either sit up here, and if I win, I won't get to go down—or I can begin walkin' like I'm going to go out to get a drink or somethin'!" Like anyone would do that with the Fan Awards on!

I just propelled myself and started walking, kinda down toward the stage, and during that walk, they called the song out as the winner, with my name as the writer.

The people who assigned seats had no clue how embarrassing it could be for a writer to have to run from the cheap seats to the stage! Roger was headed up the stairs, and I was saying, "Roger, I'm here!" I was running to catch up!

He looked around and saw me, and his little face just exploded in joy. He didn't even know I was there! He came to where I was, took my hand, and walked me up the stage. That meant so much to the both of us.

I didn't even have time to prepare what I was going to say!

It was one of those times when you're so excited you think you're going to need to have oxygen. They instantly whisk you to the back to get your picture made; all the winners were on the front of the next Singing News issue. Karen Peck Gooch and Sheri Easter were the only other ladies on the front of that magazine!

Rewind eleven years to 1984, the year we were so sure "We Shall See Jesus" was going to win song of the year. Everybody had said, "Dianne, you gotta dress to the nines, 'cause you're going to have to go up there and get that award!"

So I bought a gorgeous bronze-colored silk dress. A friend I worked with had a blond mink stole, and I borrowed it. Back then, especially, at Quartet Convention, that's how you dressed. There wasn't any of this wearing slacks and flip-flops around.

My hair was done up, and I had spiked-heel shoes on. I was so ready, I was made up, and I borrowed that stole! I suppose it was obvious to everybody that I had come to win!

Ed Hill has always been a great friend of mine; I love him dearly. We were talking that night, and he said, "You sure do look pretty, girl."

I said, "Well, thank you!"

"And I'm glad you do," he said, "'cause your song is going to win!"

"That's what everybody's saying," I replied, "but Ed, I just don't know." I'm never nervous, but I was nervous that night because I thought, "I don't know what I'm going to say!"

Everybody had me so certain I was going to win, I was almost out of my chair, and I heard them say, "Oh for a Thousand Tongues."

I thought, "I sure am dressed up to have to sit out here and lose!" That just seemed so terrible! I put in so much effort on the externals!

Besides, I had dieted, and I had the weight off. And any time I'm in a size twelve, I'm kinda full of myself anyway—that happens so rarely!

The song that won was a wonderful song, but it hasn't quite stood the test of time like "We Shall See Jesus." It didn't have the Cathedrals connection. The Cathedrals song that won for me was not up to what the other one was. So it just wasn't the time.

I guess God knew that if I was going to borrow a mink stole to win in, I wasn't mature enough in my career or in my Christianity! He probably thought, "If you're borrowing mink stoles, I don't think you're ready, Di!"

There's a whole lot of glamor girl in me, as I told you before, and I have to suppress her sometimes! When He let me win, I had on a church dress, not a mink stole!

Dianne learned her lesson! You don't borrow a mink coat, girl, or you'll be stuck to the seat like velcro!

The year I won, my weight was back up, and I had on a church dress. Think He was trying to tell me something? The Lord just has His way of keeping His little girl straight. And I'm thankful because I want to be a good steward, and I want to have the right motivations.

I had three songs on the next record they made, *Raise the Roof.*

"No News is Good News" is so much more timely now than it was then—a portent of things to come! Roger and George liked that it was really like today—what was in the newspapers. Even then, in the early- to mid-'90s, it seemed like there wasn't any good news. And it wasn't nearly as bad then as it is now! It was an up-to-date, contemporary idea for a Gospel song, and they loved that.

I've said before that nobody was ever born like Jesus, nobody ever lived like Jesus, and nobody ever died like Jesus. I wanted to put that down into a song—"Never Before and Never Again." Roger and Scott both really liked that one because they couldn't think of any other song that said what it said so plainly; they thought it was unique.

"Oh Come Along," a convention-style song I wrote, was released to the radio, and it did pretty well.

One day, Dove Brothers lead singer McCray Dove came to me and said, "Dianne, you really drove me crazy, and you didn't know it."

"Why?"

"I was lookin' through every old Stamps-Baxter songbook I had," he replied, "tryin' to find that song! I just knew they'd dug up a gem from the past that I didn't know, and I'd thought I knew all of them! And it was brand new!"

I said, "That's the best compliment I ever had!"

I was there when the Cathedrals did their *Reunion* taping in 1994, at the Roy Acuff Theatre on the Opryland Grounds. I was living just a couple of hours away at the time, so I worked most of that day, went home, and got my dressy dress and my big earrings on!

It was the only time I'd ever been in that theater. It was just an electrifying night because there they all were—Bobby Clark, George Amon Webster, Roy Tremble, and all those guys from the very beginning. They saved the lineup with Kirk Talley for last; he had such star power even then.

They sang "Oh Come Along" and "Master Builder"; they also sang "Never Before, Never Again" and "Boundless Love," but the first two were only ones on the video.

The house was packed; to sit there was like reliving the relationship and the songs and everything I'd been through with them, in a panoramic view. It was like watching it play out on the big screen.

It was just one of those golden nights. There aren't words to explain what it feels like to sit in the audience, hear those songs, and see the audience singing the words.

I drove back the same night and went to work the next morning!

At the time, nobody knew that *Faithful*, the Cathedrals' 1998 project, would be their last. Some of my songs were right there till the very last, and by a fluke, none made the final cut. Roger regretted that for the rest of his life.

I said, "Honey, don't worry, we had a great run."

When I got to Quartet Convention in 1999, Mark Trammell didn't look like he usually looked. He said, "Di, I've gotta tell you somethin', and it's really bad. Glen's in the hospital. We don't know what's wrong yet, but it's not lookin' good."

I felt like someone had knocked my legs out from under me. Glen Payne was a locomotive of a man who had never even had a bad cold! Big ole broad-shouldered thing, looked like he was born in a suit and tie, healthy as a horse, just a vibrant man.

By the end of the week, we knew what it was—cancer—and it was as bad as it could be.

So the boys were out there, knowing how sick he was, and knowing it was the sunset of the Cathedrals. My poor little Roger had to sing Glen's part.

It was about six weeks from the diagnosis to Glen's funeral.

They had intended to stay on the road till the end of '99, and Glen made them promise they would fulfill their dates. Glen and George were the consummate businessmen. You didn't fail the promoters, you didn't fail the fans; you took care of business.

Glen's illness and decline had been so rapid that I couldn't make my mind take it in. He was a robust man; he just had this marvelous way of dressing up, of looking right in a suit. In just that six weeks of time, cancer took such a toll on Glen that I don't think I would have known him. It was the hardest, hardest thing. We just weren't ready to say goodbye to Glen.

As stressful as it was for his widow, Van, she put on the perfect funeral. We overuse the word classy, but that's the way it was. The funeral was in a beautiful church, and the songs were beautiful; it was in good taste.

George Younce had been the sick one. We'd been praying for him all the way through. But he was such a comeback kid—he could be on dialysis and just pitiful one day, and the next, he would walk on stage and become George! And sing like George! And joke like George! So I thought even George would live forever. But he passed away in 2005. His funeral was in Ohio, so I wasn't able to go.

14

I loved my work in Memphis in the early '90s, but it was really too much for one person. God had a better plan.

In 1993, I got a call out of the blue from Don Wilkerson at Regional Hospital in Jackson, Tennessee. It was an HCA Hospital, a well-known national for-profit chain.

He said, "You don't know me, but I've been given your name. We've had our survey by the Joint Commission for Accreditation of Health Care Facilities, and we didn't do well in some of the areas. We're doin' the work, but we don't have it documented like they want it, and they're comin' back. I've got to have somebody that can get us prepared and pull this thing together."

I had already decided that Memphis is not a place to be a widow. I loved my condo, but it was open parking. I had the prettiest little candy-apple-red 1991 Cadillac Coup deVille Bauritz you ever saw, with a sun roof, and the folks down there intended to steal that car. It had a chip so that they couldn't hot-wire it; when they found that out, they just got mad and busted the glass out of it! That happened twice when I was living in that condo.

I thought, "I'm not stayin' down here. It's too mean, it's too big." I hadn't even thought about where I might go, but God already intervened and Don Wilkerson called. I didn't even have to look for another job!

Don was in a mood to let me negotiate, and negotiate I did! I got advice from a long-time friend who knew more about money and finances than I did. He said, "Be sure you negotiate a move out of him—make him pay for the move!"

I did, because here's what Don wanted me to do! He wanted me to leave work on a Friday at Methodist Hospital, and start in his hospital on Monday! So I said, "Then you're going to get the movin' people, and I'm not packin' a thing, and you're going to pay for every bit of it!"

He said, "Done!"

I had lost a lot of weight, was all skinny, and I had about a million clothes! I don't think that man had any *clue* how many clothes Dianne was going to move!

I found and bought a house close to the hospital and went to work. We did great on that survey, and things were rocking along.

But all the way through, I wanted to retire in Dyersburg; my brother Jim was pastoring at Springhill Baptist Church, and it was going strong. When I was living in Memphis, and then in Jackson, I'd get so lonesome for Springhill that sometimes on Sunday I'd just drive up there! I'd hear Jim preach, see my friends, and cry all the way back home. My friends at the hospital would say, "Dianne, you're never going to find a church, 'cause it's never going to match up to what you get when you go back up there!"

Out of the blue, in 1995, I got a call from Dyersburg Medical Group (now MedSouth Healthcare.) The group was a multi-specialty, multi-location group of clinics. They wanted me to set up quality assurance activities like I'd done in hospitals. They also wanted me to work on their charts because their medical records were not uniform.

But the big thing was that they didn't really understand how to code and send in their claims to Medicare and other payers, to get their optimal reimbursement and stay out of trouble. Send in false claims, and you will get in trouble! They don't teach that in medical school. They teach clinical in medical school; they don't teach financial.

When you go to the doctor, a document is generated that you carry around through the whole clinic. If you have to go to the lab, they'll circle a blood count. Maybe you have a chest x-ray. Well, eventually, you get to the doctor's office, and his charge will be circled. Then, when you get ready to check out, you turn that sheet in, and the charges that have been accumulated will eventually generate a claim. The more complex your problems are, and the more cognitive work that's required of a physician, the higher he can code by our billing system, but the documentation has to support all that.

When they called me in 1995, I said, "I don't know anything about y'all's coding, I just know hospitals', which is different."

The doctors said, "Yeah, but you'll learn it, and you know how to teach it to us." They knew I could teach it. "You know how to design forms, and how to help us have legitimate shortcuts. You're the person we need. So what'll it take to get you to come?"

I said, "Well, first of all, you can't pay me, because I negotiated so much out of those HCA people, I'd have to take a cut!"

They answered, "No, we know we're losin' so much money by codin' too low, that we'd probably pay for you in the first six months!"

And then I said, "Would you move me?"

I've spent sixteen years now, not only auditing their notes, but also creating the educational materials that I use to teach them. So I've been educating physicians all these years, and still do!

Here's how it all happened. One of the dearest doctors at MedSouth was Dr. Ralph Reynolds. Dr. Reynolds is the one who had to come and tell me that day at the hospital what was wrong with Tim, and that he probably wasn't going to get better. He was so tender-hearted, he cried telling me that.

One day, my sister-in-law saw Dr. Reynolds somewhere. Dr. Reynolds said, "Well, Sondra, how's Dianne doin' in Jackson?"

She said, "Well, she's doin' OK, but if you wanna know the truth, she'd rather be over here. She misses our church."

That's all she said. He began to ruminate on that, and then he had the idea to bring me over. So I've always thought my sister-in-law deserved a little credit for being who God used to get me back home. I started back in July of '95.

I found a house that was just right. I wanted an older house that had a living room and a den which I could make into a music room.

I've loved my whole healthcare career, but honestly, its pinnacle has been here. In the hospital, the foundation is already laid, and all the building blocks are in place. They have to be because Joint Commission's coming! You have your policies and procedures, all your documents in writing. In the physican's office setting, none of that is required, but my doctors wanted all that, so it was exciting to build it from the ground up.

I would get them around the meeting tables. We would brainstorm, developing policies and protocols. It was groundbreaking at the time; no one forced physicians to have someone like me on board. (They still don't *have* to be accredited.) They were so far ahead of the curve—they hired someone to do quality and billing compliance, when people in *Memphis* weren't doing it yet!

West Tennessee Health Care came into my life once again when my doctors developed a loose management relationship with them. They came up to Dyersburg and saw what we were doing, how the doctors had learned to code, and they said, "We need the compliance activities that Dianne is doing for you! So if you'll put her on a matrix and let us have her three days a week, we'll help you pay her, and she can teach and do what she's doin' for all these other clinics like she's doin' with y'all." What really ended up happening was that I had two full-time jobs through the mid-'90s!

In about 1997 or 1998, I realized I couldn't do it all, so I came back full time to MedSouth. But the clinics I had helped all over West and Middle Tennessee kept calling and asking if I could still come and help them.

So my doctors had a bright idea: Open a separate LLC consulting company for my services and hire someone to help me. When I traveled, we would bill for my services, and it would be like ancillary income for my physicians. They allowed me to be a partner in that company.

This is when I nearly put myself in the grave. I loved it, and I was entrepreneurial about it. I loved to get new clients, and I loved to travel—especially toward Nashville, because you *know* I'd find something to do over there! But once again, I was working too hard at something I loved. God has His ways of protecting me from that.

All of the original doctors that recruited me have retired except for one pediatrician. They're all still living, and the relationships are still sweet. I have had multitudes of career-connected friends everywhere I've worked. I've been so blessed!

God put me in this health care career long before I ever knew that I would be supporting myself from the time I was in my 40s and childless. While I am a shameless song-pitcher, I am not a shameless Dianne-pusher. God had to help get the different moves and promotions done because I would not have been that way. In retrospect, I can see so plainly!

Never once have I been in need. The music income is something He allows to help me live better than I would otherwise live. I've never had to depend on it. It's been there, and it's always been *enough*. God truly does supply the need of His child.

15

As the 1990s wound down, I realized that Glen and George were nearing retirement. I thought, "Well, what am I going to do now? Everybody knows my name, but I'm a Cathedrals songwriter."

Out of the blue, in 1996 or 1997, Phil Cross asked me to come speak at a songwriter's seminar in Nashville, with Bill Gaither and Dottie Rambo. It was a divine thing because I just wasn't in that circle. I could have understood him inviting someone who was huge at the time, like Squire Parsons or Ronny Hinson!

I hadn't been acquainted with Phil before that. He was a big Cathedrals fan—he wrote "Champion of Love"—and knew my music by then. God put me in the right place at the right time.

The day I spoke, Phil said, "There are writers in this room who are not artists. And you writers don't even know who each other are!" So he went around the room and had us stand up, and list off five of our songs that we'd written. Of course, everybody will say their biggest ones—vanity of vanities, all is vanity!

Afterwards, here came a young man I didn't know, walking towards me. He looked like a college professor or someone brilliant from academia. He said, "You're Dianne Wilkinson? I'm Niles Borop, of Centergy Music."

I had heard of Centergy. Daryl Williams was with them, and he had told me that all they did was publish. They just lived to pitch your songs and get your demos made. I couldn't believe it—I thought, "Oh, my goodness, you don't mean it!"

I was still just green. I didn't live in that world. It was a peripheral world to my world. I was a healthcare gal. I had a career; I had family; I had a whole other life.

I had told Daryl, "I don't know what kinda luck I'd have doing that, 'cause everybody that does my songs has got their own publishing! And they're used to doing mine on a song by song basis!"

And he said, "Oh, this deal would be better."

Well, Niles began to talk to me. "Let's just see how it works. You don't have to sign an exclusive; just send a song along and I'll see what I can do." I sent a little song called "Sweet Glory Land," which Perfect Heart cut, when Jeff Stice was with them.

I sent a few more along, and we began to get acquainted. The year "Oh Come Along" was nominated for a Dove Award, we went to a BMI reception honoring the most-played songs on Southern Gospel radio that year. He introduced me to people from the industry who were there, and our relationship began to grow. I could tell he really knew a lot about music and publishing.

In 1999 or 2000, he began asking me to sign an exclusive contract with Centergy. I was concerned about that because everyone who cut my songs had their own publishing. Roger Bennett had his own publishing. Gold City cut "I've Passed Over into Canaanland" and "Longing for Beulah Land" when Mark Trammell was handling their publishing. Greater Vision, with Gerald Wolfe, cut "He is Mine" and "Of Thee I Sing."

Roger was the one I was most worried about because he was really the one I was closest to all the way through. I thought, "Roger is going to fall down on the floor and do an act. He's going to cry these great big crocodile tears, and work me like a plow mule, and make me think I can't sign so he can still have all the publishing! He's going to pull out all the stops!"

This is the way I put it to Niles: "Man, do we have to get married? Why can't we just go steady? What are my boys going to think?"

He said, "Your boys will take the songs if they're good enough, and they'll be good enough. They won't care about the publishing."

I began to pray about it. The Lord really led me to sign with Niles because I knew that Niles could broaden my work out there to artists that I wasn't that familiar with. I knew that he had a great chance of getting my stuff in print; that's where a lot of the money was back then. As a widow by then, I had to think about the business aspect. He was still going to let me pitch to my guys that I had relationships with. The Lord just led me to know, "This is the best chance you've got right here. You've got someone who is going to work hard for you, and this is what you should do."

So I just told the boys, "I've prayed about it, and this is what the Lord wants me to do."

Roger and several of the others just said: "I don't care who's got the publishing as long as I get the songs!"

I was playing piano for my own song demos back then; Terry Franklin did the vocals. Niles liked my piano style; he would have me come over when we had six or eight to do. He had the studio right there in his office suite. Looking back, I don't know if that was the greatest thing, but it saved some money, and at least I got them like I wanted them. I knew where to voice Terry, to get the best of his range. And they were getting cut right and left!

At this point, Rebecca Peck was with Niles. Her husband Tom came to work there. Niles had several staffers, like Tom, and later Rick Shelton, do a lot of the pitching to artists. Niles saved himself to interact with the writers, really manage them, and meet their needs. He was great at that. He loved to mentor new writers who had talent but were green; I have never met anyone who could do that as well as he could.

One golden night, I went to the BMI awards event with Niles, and he introduced me to Rick Shelton. He said, "Guess what, Dianne, I've pulled Rick out of radio. He worked for Solid Gospel, and he's going to work with Centergy." Rick and I were instantly fast friends. He's a precious young man, a preacher's kid; he's a good, good man.

I suppose I could have stayed endlessly at Centergy till Jesus came. I loved everybody there. Niles worked hard for me and I did my thing. We had a great team.

This went on till 2005. But some of their long-standing writers moved on, and Niles had to downsize. He eventually closed up shop at Centergy and went on to other career endeavors. He helped Rick Shelton get the job at Daywind Music Publishing.

I was very close to Rick, and he asked me to join Daywind as an exclusive writer. I prayed about it, and the Lord led me to Daywind. I signed with them in late 2005.

The Lord blessed; I was still getting Kingdom Heirs, Gold City, and Legacy Five cuts, and I finally began to get some Kingsmen cuts.

My relationship with Rick Shelton makes Daywind special to me. I trust him to have the conversations and protect the relationships with the artists who mean so much to me, and treat them fairly about my songs. We work well together, and it's been a great relationship.

16

One night in 1999, out of the blue, my phone rang. I heard an East Tennessee accent: "Dianne, this is Steve French, Kingdom Heirs. You don't know me. I just thought I'd tell you we just cut your song today."

I had heard of the Kingdom Heirs. In 1986, they became the resident Gospel group at Dollywood, in Pigeon Forge, Tennessee. However, I didn't know Steve at the time. So I just said, "Which one?"

He added, "Well, Gold City never done nothin' with 'I've Passed Over into Canaanland,'" and it just kinda laid on their record, and they never sent it to radio. But we've always loved it, and we just cut it, and we're going to send it to the radio!"

I said, "Well, honey, help yourself!"

And then, he said, "What else have you got? We liked that one so well, send us something else!"

I was just beginning to write for Centergy, and I had some new ones. I put some on a disc, and mailed them to him. I didn't think much more about it.

When they sent me that CD, *The Journey Home*, and I heard how great they did "I've Passed Over." I was *so* excited! I knew the Kingdom Heirs were a good quartet, but the measure for me of a good quartet is "What are they going to do with my song?" They just killed it—it was just great!

A year later, I get another call. "Dianne, this is Steve French. We just cut five of the songs you sent me!"

The album was titled after one of the five, "City of Light."

"Do You Know What it Means (To Be a Child of the King)" is the bluesy kind that lead singer Arthur Rice loves so well. N'Harmony had also cut that one. "Salvation is the Miracle to Me" is the song that Legacy Five cut on their debut project; the Kingdom Heirs didn't care if someone else had done it, they'd do it anyway! They also cut "Common Little Things" and "God Made It."

Gonna Keep Telling (2002) included three of my songs, "Nobody Knows the Answer but God," "I'm Gonna Keep Praising Jesus' Name," and "He'll See You Through."

"He'll See You Through" is one of my favorite things they ever did. I don't remember what prompted me to write it, but their version of it was absolutely flawless. The riffs that Jeff Stice plays in there are some of the most unbelievable piano work he has ever done. That year at Quartet Convention, they did it every time they hit the stage. Forget that it's my song; their performance was the best thing I heard that year. They were spot-on, they were tight; it was perfection. I just loved the cut.

From "I've Passed Over" till now, *Going on With the Song* is their only mainline record that I didn't get anything on. For some reason, I didn't hear from Steve, and I didn't know that they were cutting. It was just one of those flukey things.

I wondered if the run was over; by then, I already knew that I loved the way they did my songs! Of course it wasn't, but you never know how it's going to shake out.

When the Kingdom Heirs were in the studio cutting *Forever Changed*, Steve called me and told me they needed one more song. "Have you got anything?"

I said, "I do!" I sang "Lord, I Always Know That I Can Count on You" over the phone.

I had written it on my way to a Kingsmen concert at Englewood Baptist Church in Jackson, Tennessee. I started getting "In the morning, in the evening," and it just started coming. And I finished it before I ever went into the church!

I got it to him quickly, and they recorded it.

They picked up two of mine for their 2005 project, *Give Me the Mountain*. I co-wrote "So Long and Goodbye" with Jerry Kelso. I really love writing with him; he writes quartet songs so well.

We both wrote for Centergy at the time. We were in a writing session together, out in Franklin, at Centergy. We had it almost finished, but not quite. We said, "Well, we'll both work on it and see if we can finish it in a couple of days." He called me the next day and had the rest of it!

If somebody said, "Dianne, we're going to pull a gun on you, and we're going to shoot you unless you tell us your favorite Arthur vocal of all time"—it's like they're all at least fifteen on a scale of one to ten, but I would have to say "Pray for Me" is just a tiny bit ahead of all the others. I think his vocal on this is absolutely perfection.

"Pray for Me" had been sent to Ernie Haase. Ernie put it on hold. I'm not sure of the timing because I apparently thought it was still free. I sent it to Steve, and he put it on hold. Bottom line, they both had it on hold which is never supposed to happen.

The versions are quite different; Lari Goss produced Signature Sound's version; there was a little bluesy harmony going on in the chorus, almost Beach Boys type. Arthur's was, of course, traditional quartet.

Two powerhouse quartets did the song; it's been great for both of them all these years. Arthur did it for years and years, and he got to where he did it with just the piano.

I play compilation CDs of my songs often to listen to the older ones, as a form of educating myself, to see what made it work and if it still works. To this day, when I hear the opening strains of "Pray For Me," I know ahead of time that I'm going to hit rewind!

The Kingdom Heirs cut eight of my songs on *True to the Call* (2007). I never dreamed I'd get eight on one project!

At the Quartet Convention before the Kingdom Heirs went into the studio, Arthur was excited about all the songs. But he looked at me with a far-off look in his eyes, and said, "You know what? 'What We Needed' will be the hit on this one."

It was my first #1 with the Kingdom Heirs. It reached #1 in July 2008.

I had seen the movie *Cold Mountain*, a civil war drama starring Nicole Kidman and Jude Law. There was a scene in that movie when they're in a little mountain town in North Carolina. They were singing in a little white frame church.

In the plot line, this was the occasion where someone came whooping in on a horse, "They've declared war!" The boys got all excited.

But they were singin' a song, and it was an old, old hymn. They were keeping the beat with their right hand. The song was,

And I don't have to stay here long

Oh, yes, my Lord, and I...

I was going, "Oh, I like that!"

I got online and did some investigating. The singing was really being done by the Sacred Harp singers. They're the people who are keeping the shape note thing going.

I got a phone number and called. An elderly gentleman picked up the phone. I was trying to get the hymnal that had that song. He said, "Yes, ma'am, I got it right here. It's so much money; you send a check, I'll send it to you."

I thought, "God love him, he doesn't even do the credit card thing!"

Well, I got it, and it's full of that kind of song.

"What We Needed" was the next song I wrote after that:

We have never seen all through history

How a man could save himself

I know it was inspired by my love for that style; I will always believe that hymn influenced "What We Needed."

And then, I thought, "We've gotta change gears in the chorus. We've gotta quartet this thing into high gear."

When I got the demo in, I thought: "This is one of the greatest demos Terry Franklin's ever done." And I knew in my soul the Kingdom Heirs would take it.

When it got down to the final selection, it was in the list. Arthur told me, "It's going to be a big song, I just know it."

One of his friends called him and said, "You really should put a warning on that song: 'Do not listen while driving.'"

I thought, "Oh, I like that!" And it's true!

I went to Frank Arnold's Songfest in Jackson, Tennessee, in 2005. After the concert, Roger Talley was asking me for songs. "Lord, Your Word Is Still True" was my latest one at the time.

I was singing the song to him, and I was two or three lines away from finishing it.

I began to feel the same sensation that I felt when I had my first heart attack, two years earlier. It wasn't as pronounced. It's very hard to describe that sense of heaviness all around your shoulders, but I felt it.

And, so help me, when I knew good and well I was having another heart attack, I went ahead and finished the song!

I knew that it wasn't to the place where I was in danger. And even as I was singing it, I was getting a game plan in my mind. I knew my car was parked close to the building, and I knew I could get to the car before I alarmed a bunch of people.

The auditorium is not that far from the hospital. I just had one of those moments of complete confidence from the Lord that I could make it fine. So I walked calmly to the car, drove myself over to the hospital, and walked in.

The first EKG was non-diagnostic, and the first set of labs was also not diagnostic. But the second set was positive. So I really did have another heart attack, but I wasn't even in ICU. It did more initial damage to my heart than the first one did, but my heart repaired itself.

When I contacted Roger Talley about that song later on, I said, "The least you can do is cut the song, Roger Talley! That's the least you can do!"

He laughed!

On later occasions, when he has asked me for songs, he says, "But I don't want you to sing me one; I'm scared of that!"

So I sent "Lord, Your Word Is Still True" to Steve French, and he put it on hold for the *True to the Call* project. Well, on this particular day, when he called to tell me, I had seven songs on the record. I was just ecstatic. They had a ballad—a Jerry Salley song, and I didn't know Jerry Salley then. They got in the studio, and it just wasn't working for them. That happens sometimes. Billy Hodges was with them, and it was a tenor lead. So they were stuck.

Steve said, "Well, let's pick up this little Dianne song." Well, Billy sang it like an angel, so they decided to do it instead.

So the day he called me, he said, "I made a mistake about saying you had seven."

I said, "Which one didn't make it?"

He said, "You have *eight*!"

I said, "You don't mean it!"

"Yes, we're doing 'Lord, Your Word Is Still True.'"

One Sunday morning, my brother preached on Titus. Titus was over on Crete with the barbarians and the slow-bellies. In other words, he was serving in a hard place. I'm sure he would have loved to be serving somewhere else!

Jim made the remark, "You know, Titus was between a rock and a hard place over there in Crete."

And I thought, "No, the Rock's between the hard place and you." I'll be honest, I almost started shaking right there in the front seat, 'cause I just knew what a hook I had. So I wrote it down on the bulletin. That's what I'd always do when Jim was preaching; I'd grab the bulletin and jot it down. The church people started noticing when I would do that. I tried to be really smooth and discreet! That afternoon, sure enough, I finished it up.

By then, when it was time to record, I made a disc of everything they were holding to send to Steve. Steve's wife Sheri has a marvelous ear for what will work. They would get out in the car, ride around the East Tennessee foothills, and listen to the CD.

They played that song. It was about to go to the next one when Sheri said, "Steve, I think you need to play that one again; that song is about Titus." I hadn't included that information, but she could tell from the lyrics that it was about Titus. She knows her Bible!

When he played it the second time, he listened harder, and he fell in love with it. Sure enough, it was the first single off of that record, and it won a BMI award for the most played song. It sat on the chart a long time.

The last time I sent him a disc for their most recent record, I said, "By the way, it's time to take Sheri out in the car, 'cause the disc is in the mail!"

I still owe her a bouquet of flowers because I know I've gotten cuts because of the ear she has!

"True to the Call" started coming to me when I was on my way over to Hendersonville, Tennessee to write. I began to get this image of a little boy playing preacher, making a little cardboard pulpit, and putting the kids out in front to be the congregation. I borrowed from Ivan Parker's testimony; he was a preacher's kid. As a little boy, he'd make all the neighborhood kids sit out in his yard, and he would get up and preach.

As the song began to develop, of course, I got the boy to where he was saved, and it just kind of came together. Then I got him through his life.

The very next day, while that song was in progress, I heard on the radio that Dr. Adrian Rogers had passed away. He was one of my lifetime heroes. I couldn't believe that he passed away while I was writing that song. I began to think about some preachers who had been so dear in my life; of course, I thought of my brother first.

When Steve heard it, he just fell in love with it. He wanted to sing it himself.

I had sent it to McCray Dove before Steve put it on hold. McCray wanted to do it so bad, he called Steve and tried to talk him out of it. Steve said, "I ain't talkin'; I ain't dealing or nothin', I'm sorry!"

They parted friends. Every now and then, a guy will call another guy, and say, "How much do you want that song—I want it bad! Are you high on it, or are you just thinking you might do it?"

The line that really touched Steve was "If he thought about quitting, no one ever knew."

When he sang the song, he couldn't believe how many preachers came up to him and said, "That's exactly my story."

So many people came and bought that CD because they wanted to take it home and give it to their pastor. It had a huge impact on people even though it was not a huge song that they did every time. In fact, I've never heard them do it in person. They don't do it on all their programs. But when they do, Steve has all the preachers in the audience come up and stand by the stage, so he can sing it to them to honor them.

When you hear preachers sitting around at preacher's conferences, they'll talk about how many times they thought about quitting. But that's because they're talking to each other. Nobody else ever knows.

Until *True to the Call* came out, I never dreamed I'd get eight cuts on a Kingdom Heirs record. And I never dreamed I'd get nine until *When You Look at Me*! They cut "On the Gloryland Way," "Biblically Correct," "Help Me, Lord," "Fire Away," "As Good as I Can Be," "Steppin' on the Stars," "When the Story of My Life Is Told," "Jesus Showed Up," and "When You Look at Me."

The title track shares my testimony. I was teaching Sunday School one morning, and I was telling my class what they saw when they looked at me. I said, "You're seeing a gal that's middle-aged, and too plump, and has to wear glasses, and has to color her hair"— I don't know how long I went on with all that.

But I said, "That's not what God sees. What you see is not the real me; the real me is what He sees."

Later in the day, I began to reflect on what the Lord sees when He looks at me. I got to thinking about the glorious transaction that made that possible. Then I thought about Him getting rid of the rags of my sin and clothing me with the righteousness of the Lord Jesus. If you're truly saved, and you ever get to pondering it, it is glorious!

I didn't know it was over six minutes long until I got the demo back. I almost fainted, because when I listen to it, I don't think of it as being that long. I thought, "Well, it'll die because nobody will ever do it."

I included it on the iPod I brought to Quartet Convention one year. Arthur just sat on the couch and scrolled through the whole thing. It never occurred to me that he would slow down at that song.

I could see him getting emotional. I wasn't sure what he was listening to. I put my head over a little closer, and then I could hear enough to know he was listening to "Far back in time / Your love all sublime"—the first part of that first verse.

He kind of teared up. I've never seen Arthur do that; he's a pretty self-contained guy. He was just so moved by that song. He listened all the way through, took the earbuds out of his ears, and said, "Dianne, that's the best thing you've ever done. The best thing you've ever done; musically, content, every other way."

I said, "Well, Hon, I'm so glad you love it. It's my testimony song."

He said, "It's mine, too. I want to hold it, and we're going to do it."

I said, "Well, what can we cut out, 'cause it's too long."

He said, "We're not gonna cut *anything*."

I didn't know how the other guys would feel about it, but Steve told me that when they would first perform it, it moved the people. And it moved Arthur; that song touched him in a deep place.

He said that when they would do the Dollywood programs, "Sometimes we do 'When You Look at Me' and 'He Locked the Gates,' and sometimes we do 'He Locked the Gates' and then close out with that one. But whichever way you do it, that's the end of the program; there's nothing that can follow that. It's over then."

It wasn't even a power ballad. It was a slow ballad—not the sort of song they do. But it just resonated with the audiences.

That song touches Arthur like no other, to this day. And you can tell when he sings it.

Well, we got on a roll. After eight on *True to the Call* and nine on *When You Look at Me*, they cut ten on *We Will Stand Our Ground!*

The project's first single was "Tell Me Why." Usually, we're trying to witness to the lost person, and we initiate the conversation. I know there's bound to be people who have questions about things they've heard about the Lord. So I thought, "What if this unsaved person is asking the questions and actually opening the door for someone to witness to them?"

I've never been in journalism class, but I know that one of the huge things they teach you about an article is to answer the questions who, what, when, where, and why. I thought, that would really make a good opener for the lost person, "I want to know all about it, and here's what I want to know. Tell me why, tell me where."

I thought, "Well, I'll take him to a saved friend."

It rocked on; I liked the groove I was getting. I got to the second verse, and this was my challenge: I thought, "Okay, Sis, you gotta answer the questions, and you got one verse to do it in! And all those people who write in on SouthernGospelBlog.com are going to say, 'She never did tell when!' They watch for that kind of thing!"

When you're crafting a song, whatever you joke with yourself about, you cover those bases. You can't have a song that says "Tell me why, tell me when," and leave something unanswered. That's the reason 'A.D. 33' is in there, and that's the reason it tells exactly where they were when the Cross event took place, and Who it was, and why. I made sure I covered all those bases.

And then, of course, my other burden was to save myself room to get this man right with God because I wanted it to end that way. Rusty Golden tells me that an official tag has to be the last line or two of what you just sang; he says that's the only way you can call it a tag. So instead of putting an official tag on the end of my song, I like putting in a closer, something totally different to leave in their minds. This time, it was so neat to be able to say, "Well, I'm glad I asked, 'cause I found out / Just what salvation is all about."

Arthur was holding a lot of my songs at the time. When we would email back and forth, he was talking about "Where's John," "We Will Stand Our Ground," and some of the others, but he never mentioned much about this song.

The night that they got the final mix on all twelve songs, Arthur emailed my ten over the period of an evening. I was in the process of listening to them, and I had just listened to "Tell Me Why" and two or three others. My phone rang, and it was Arthur. He said, "Which one do you like the best so far?"

I said, "Well, it's a real tough call for me, but so far, I think the best thing I've heard is 'Tell Me Why!'"

He started giggling.

I said, "What are you giggling about?"

He said, "You know how I hadn't been saying anything about that song?"

I said, "Yeah!"

He said, "Well, it's my favorite one on the record! After I heard the final thing, I just loved the way it came out."

Steve called me not long after that. By that time I had listened to all of them. It was my personal favorite—not necessarily the song, since it's like picking among your children to name a favorite song, but the way the cut came out! I really loved the cut!

He asked me which one I liked the best, and I said "Tell Me Why."

He said, "Oh! That's the first single!"

The second single was the title track, "We Will Stand Our Ground." One Sunday morning, my brother preached a sermon about the fundamentals of our faith and the importance of preserving them. I began to think about a phrase we have used a lot in talking about this subject, "contending for the faith." I recognized my thought process as one that was leading to writing a song.

Jude 1:3 expressed my feelings so well: "Beloved, when I gave all diligence to write unto you of the common salvation, it was needful for me to write unto you, and exhort you that ye should earnestly **contend for the faith** which was once delivered unto the saints." He goes on to describe ungodly men who were "turning the grace of our God into lasciviousness and denying the **only Lord God** and **our Lord Jesus Christ**" (emphasis is mine).

That afternoon, all I could think about was how very true that is *today* with so many false religions in the world which are gaining in strength and numbers and even getting converts from Christianity. We've always known that in the last days the Church would be under attack; but I don't know that Christians where I live ever thought we might actually have to be Christian *soldiers*. But I think we do indeed have to be, because there are things worth holding on to at any cost. I wanted to write this as encouragement and as a clarion call to the people of God.

As often happens with songs that are coming to me, the words and music came together, and in this case, the first verse came first. In the crafting process, I wanted to be sure to state clearly the things that *were* worth fighting for and never compromising about. They are in the chorus: The Book, and the blood, and the rugged cross.

I wanted the song to be able to speak to people everywhere who either believe in a false religion, or a false "gospel" such as Paul spoke about, which means any gospel besides GRACE. Yes, I'm a fundamentalist...and I'm prepared to take the heat for that. The title of the song says what I feel the most passionate about these days relating to my faith: "We Will Stand Our Ground." And as God told Elijah, He will always have a remnant of folks who *will*—even if it's a small remnant in comparison to how many people there are in the world!

When I first wrote it, the political situation in this country was not in my mind at all. I was thinking about contending for the faith. But looking back, I can see so plainly how the Lord could use it in that other direction.

I had a stunning demo on the song and sent it to one of the quartets with whom I have a huge track record. They put it on hold but passed on it. I was surprised because as we writers say, it "sounded just like them."

Later on, when the Kingdom Heirs were looking for songs, I almost didn't send this one because they just don't do ballads. They make a few exceptions (like "When You Look at Me"). But I felt the Lord was leading me to send it to Arthur, and he put it on hold. Later on when he notified me of final song selections, this song was on the list.

When Steve French talked to me about the songs, he said that this one was on the list to record from the first time they heard it because they felt it was a message the Church needed to hear. I was thrilled because they sing to huge numbers of people every year, and I knew—as He always does—that God gets the right songs to the right groups.

When I heard the final mix of the song with the beautiful orchestration and the perfection of the vocals, it was very moving. I prayed right then that the Lord would use this song to encourage believers in these perilous times in which we live.

As to the way the Kingdom Heirs sing my songs, I am *always* delighted with the finished recording because I know how high their standards are when they get ready to go into the studio and how hard they work to "get it right." They're great singers and musicians, and they have a genius at the creative helm in Arthur Rice as producer.

When *We Will Stand Our Ground* was coming out, I wasn't dreading anything but "Where's John." I was thinking, "People are either going to think it's a great song, or they're going to think I've lost my mind. One of the two. There's not going to be any middle ground about this song!"

I had not sat down and planned to write this song. It's the oddest thing. I started singing that line, "Something's happening, folks are going crazy / I'm hearing talk about outer space."

I thought, "Oh, a rapture song."

And then I thought, "The guy's been left." Then the cemetery line just flowed in there.

I don't remember having the title at first, but somehow, when I wrote the line about how all the lights are on, it made it really easy to make the brother's name John.

After I got the first verse done, I thought, "Okay, nobody's ever written a Gospel song just like this. It's so obvious that someone is not only left behind but desperate. But I've got to have this person's fear mount as the song goes on. I've got to have him get more and more desperate."

As that realization hit me, I thought, "I'm going to write myself right out of a cut here because if I make it like I know it has to be, no one will ever cut it. Everybody's saying, 'We want a happy song, and there's nothing happy about it!'"

And I thought, "Lord, I know if You're giving me this, I know You're giving it to me for a reason, so I'm just going to follow Your lead, and we're going to finish it out."

It didn't take all that long to write, and if you follow it all the way through and look back to the beginning, you can see that his fear is growing. "Now I see many people are missing..."

I put it in a minor key on purpose. At that point, there's no way to make it happy. I don't know how a lot of people believe, but this is my belief system: The Bible says that God Himself will send people a strong delusion, after the Rapture, that they'll believe the lie, the Antichrist. So I sensed that this man had heard and had a chance to be saved before. So there is no good end for this man, in my doctrinal system of belief. Even Tim LaHaye believes this man could be saved, but see, if God sends the delusion, they're not going to call on the name of the Lord. That's what I believe. I think that once the Rapture comes, it's too late for those who had heard the Gospel before. I didn't have to get into what I believe; I just wrote the song.

I thought its only value is if it jars someone into making their decision now. It's clear that a lot of people that have never been saved have heard of the Rapture. When I was a kid, people didn't talk about it. Everyone knows about it now.

So I thought, "If the message needs to get out there, who's going to record it?"

This is the most amazing part of this story: The young man who did the track, Adam Kohout from North Carolina, gets the musicians in the studio to get the full band sound. From what Rick Shelton told me, it was Adam's idea to send it to Arthur Rice to do demo vocals. I don't know why; Arthur has never demoed a song of mine before.

So when the demo came in, and I heard Kingdom Heirs bass singer Jeff Chapman singing, I thought, "Jeff Chapman!" And then I heard Arthur, and I thought, "Arthur's done the demo!"

I emailed Rick back and I said, "This is great, but I'm curious—how did this get to Arthur?"

He said, "Well, I'm not sure; it was Adam's idea, and I just said okay."

And I thought, "This is just too weird. It's a weird song, and this is a weird event! Something is going on that's bigger than I am."

I felt sure that if Arthur had had any interest in that song at all, he would have put it on hold. When I didn't hear from him, I thought, "Well, there went my only hope of anybody cutting it because I didn't hear back from Arthur. But of course, it's not their kind of song. It's not."

I thought nobody would ever do it!

But here's what I did think of doing: "I would love for Steve to hear how great his boys did this demo because it's different from what they do. So Steve would get a kick out of hearing this because it's not a Kingdom Heirs kind of song."

So I sent it to him. Honestly, in my mind, it was not a pitch because I didn't dream they'd do it. This is what I emailed Steve: "Just give a listen to what your guys did on this demo. I know it's not y'all's kind of song, but I want you to hear how great they did it."

Well, he called me back, right after he got it, and he said, "Who's got that song? Who's got it?"

I said, "Well, nobody's got it, and nobody will, I don't think!"

He said, "Oh, I'm up here in the airport"—it was the Indianapolis airport—"I'm listening to it on my iPhone, these other people can hear it, and it's drawing a crowd! I'm telling you, this song has got to be done; this message has got to get out to people! I want to put it on hold. Consider it recorded!"

Well, I almost fell off of my little computer chair because I wasn't expecting that to happen!

Of course, I knew that Jeff would do this one because he did the demo, and he did it so well.

They sing every day at Dollywood to people who are unchurched, who just walk in for a place to sit for a while.

All the Rapture songs I've heard have been anticipatory; I've never heard a Rapture song with a message like that.

Honestly, I have not had any negative comments. I have had some people tell me they think it's the best thing on the record. I think maybe that's because it is so different.

From 1999 through today, the Kingdom Heirs have cut forty of my songs. It's just a phenomenon that they can't explain, and I can't explain.

One time, Kingdom Heirs bass singer Jeff Chapman told me, "Dianne, your writing has changed the course of the Kingdom Heirs. It's taken 'em to a new place." He meant stylistically, without changing the fact that it's quartet all the way.

Whatever lineup they have, Steve and Arthur are the George and Glen of today. They are the core. Whatever the lineup, it's still going to be Kingdom Heirs.

17

My life changed forever in 2001. That's the year that my family's carefree days left forever.

My mother had lived alone for a long time, but she had become weak in her legs. We thought the problem was arthritis since she had arthritis in her knees. She was still living in the family house; after Grandmother died in 1976, Mama bought out her three siblings' share of the house and property and kept living there.

She worked for a wonderful, Godly man who ran an insurance agency. She became a licensed agent and worked there for thirty years until she retired in the '80s. She stayed in the house by herself through the '80s and '90s. The house needed some repairs that it never did get, but she didn't care. She was always comforted and never afraid in that old house.

She had gotten to the place where she was prone to falling, so I talked to her every single day or night. I had made an appointment to go with her to the doctor because I thought, "This has to be something more than arthritis."

One night in July 2001, I fell asleep in my chair and woke up at 3:00 in the morning. I didn't try to call Mama till the next day. But I couldn't reach her on the phone. It's just a forty-minute trip, so instead of calling someone, I drove over. I was uneasy, but I still thought it would be okay. Of course, I had a key.

Mama had fallen the day before, and she couldn't get up or get to a telephone. For some reason, the air conditioning wasn't working, and since this was in the summertime, the house was so hot she was dehydrated. I called the ambulance.

She had hit her head, but she was not seriously injured. We got her to the hospital. Bottom line, she had a profound vitamin B12 deficiency, which her regular doctor had not noticed. I can't believe that he never suggested, "Why are the legs weak?"

We knew then that she couldn't continue to live alone. She didn't want to leave Blytheville because she loved her friends, and she loved her church. She was still going to Ridgecrest, the church my family helped found. She really got worse, so we moved her to Dyersburg. She moved in with my brother Jim and his wife Sondra. (Sondra doesn't work outside the home, and I worked in a career with a lot of travel involved.)

When we found out she needed to move, we knew we were going to be faced with selling the house.

"Family home" doesn't begin to say what it meant to me. This was the house my granddaddy built in the '40s. We moved into it after my mother's divorce, and I lived there till I got married.

It was where Grandmother taught me about Jesus and where she sent me for my first piano lesson. So there was just something about that place. I loved every blade of grass growing there!

No one expects to have to do the final cleanup at your family home while your parent is still alive. Mama wasn't able to be a part of that. It was a sad thing because we didn't want to have to sell the house. We didn't want Mama to have to move; she didn't want to move. She moved because she lost her independence.

Jim and I would go to the house on Saturdays. There was an immense amount of things to pack. Some of the people, including me, who had lived there still had things back in the bedrooms. Mama mainly lived in one part, and didn't really go in those other rooms often. She was a bit of a packrat anyway—though we found some real treasures in the things she kept.

Mama moved over here in 2001, and it took us a while to find a buyer for the house. As it turns out, her sweet neighbors, the Purdues, bought it for their son. They were a black family; they were church people, and they were precious!

Mr. Purdue was a big, strong fellow. When they first moved in, he knocked on Mama's door, and he said, "Ma'am, it appears to me that you live alone over here, and I want you to know that we wanna be good neighbors to you. I don't care what you need from my family, all you have to know is to knock on the door or give us a call; I'll help you any time."

They watched after my mother as tenderly as if she had been theirs. In fact, when she fell and was hospitalized, he came to the hospital and was crying outside her room. His great big shoulders were shaking. I said, "Oh! Please don't cry!"

He said, "I wasn't there for Miss Blanche. I know she called me, and I couldn't hear."

I said, "Oh, Mr. Purdue, she wouldn't want you to feel bad."

Mr. Purdue and his wife bought the house, knowing the shape it was in. They took it as is, which had to be a God thing. It sold for more than we thought it would, and it was bought by people who loved my mother.

I think it was 2003 before the house sold. We were going through the business of doing the final cleaning and getting ready to transfer the keys. Aunt Mavis had died that year. I also had my first heart attack earlier that year, so I couldn't do as much of the heavy lifting as I would have been able to do before.

The day came when we had finished all the work, and we knew this was the day to turn the key over. I was on my way up there to help my brother do the final cleanup. My heart was all the way down in my knees. I thought, "I don't think I can do it, I just don't think I can."

Grandmother always had a showplace of a yard. How she had time to do all that, run a beauty shop, and half the time, get dinner on the table, nobody knows. She could multi-task before anybody knew what that was and make it look easy! She had the most beautiful trees and flowers.

I was thinking, "How can I leave this yard, when she planted everything in it?" I cried a while, and thought, "Well, what will I do if I get over there and I can't keep it together? I can't let my brother see me in this shape, or he can't do it either!"

I was focusing on the boards, the nails, and the roof. And the Lord reminded me that I had to focus on Him, not the boards or the nails.

The words to the song "This Old Place" began coming to me. With that song, the Lord got me to focus on the people in that house who were waiting for me. I got the whole song before getting there. It got me through that afternoon. I absolutely believe that if He hadn't given me that song, I couldn't have done it.

The Purdues stayed in touch with Mama, so in a way, she still felt a part of "This Old Place." All my family feels that way.

I had no intention of pitching "This Old Place." It was *way* too personal. I made a Gospel song out of it, but it was really about my homeplace. It was so personal that I almost didn't send it to Niles Borop at Centergy. I told him about it, and he said, "No, just send it, just send it."

When I played it for him, he said, "Oh yes, ma'am, we're going to pitch it. There's too many people who have lived this song, and if they haven't, they're going to."

This is back when I was playing my own demos. It was just a simple Dianne / Terry Franklin demo, and he sang it from his heart as only Terry can.

Ernie Haase totally got it when I sent them that song. He said, "That song touches me, because I've *lived* that song." He recorded it on the album he released after George Younce—his father-in-law—passed away. He sang it like an angel. And through the years he sang the song, he always introduced it as his tribute to George.

I still get emails from people about that song. I thought, "I was so wrong!" Everyone will live "This Old Place." You've already lived it, or you will. Niles was right.

I got an email from a lady who said, "We're about to have to tear down our church because we're going to have to rebuild. We don't believe we can stand it. We know the church is not the bricks, but we just don't think we can stand it. We would like to use your song in our program to build our new church because we think it'll help us get through it."

I thought, "Well, what a good idea, to apply it to the church." And I replied, "I'm honored, and I hope you will, but I want you to let me know how it goes."

Later on, she emailed me: "We broke ground. It's goin' up, and it was a happy occasion, and not a sad occasion, because we were able to focus on the people, on their influence, and where they were." She said, "I don't think we could have done it without that song."

So to say it's special—there's no way to describe it.

My mother passed away in 2010. Grandmother, Aunt Mavis, and Mama taught me my work ethic. You go to work, you do the very best you can and have your own standards for yourself. You show up every day, on time, unless there is an unbelievably strong reason not to be there. You work in a way that makes people know they can *count* on you.

Mama was smart, multi-talented, and could do anything she put her hand to. She was an amazing singer, sewed beautiful dresses for me without a pattern, decorated cakes and Easter eggs like nobody else ever did, and wrapped the prettiest Christmas packages in the world.

She was great fun and had a multitude of friends. She was a champ athlete all her life, and when Blytheville got its only bowling lanes she took to bowling like a fish to water. The last couple of years she bowled in league, she had to bowl in the men's league because she had zero handicap and couldn't really bowl with the women anymore. More often than not, she beat the *men*.

And if she couldn't make you laugh, you just had a *problem*. She had personality with a capital "P." My mother was my best friend, my confidante, and the person who loved me more than anyone else ever will. I miss her so much, but I'll see her again!

When I was younger, I taught younger people in Sunday School. But I now teach the Open Door Sunday School Class at

Springhill Baptist Church in Dyersburg. We call it open door because anyone is welcome; we've got some young married people in there, we've got some old married people in there, we've got couples, we've got singles, we've got ladies whose husbands don't come, so we say, "Come one, come all."

I really have three callings on my life—that's one, the songwriting is one, and the Lord called me to be a church musician. I still play piano for my church, three times a week. I love to do that. I don't bail out on my church to go to singings.

It's just an amazing thing, that you fall in love with what God calls you to do! And that's not any accident, is it?

18

Tim and I lived across the river from Memphis when Clayton Inman was still singing with his brothers as The Inmans. Clayton's son, Scotty, was a little bitty toddler. He was a stocky little guy, with blond curls and big ol' china blue eyes, the most darling little boy. I didn't have children; he took up with me just like that, and I would beg Clayton and his wife to give him to me; I wanted him so bad!

Well, he grew up and joined Triumphant Quartet. I remember seeing them early on in Alabama; Scotty came to me and said, "Miss Dianne, I'm trying to get started writing. Will you help me?"

I had not co-written with anybody prior to this. Could I look at that little sweet face and say, "I've never been co-writing, and I don't think I'm going to like it?"

So I said, "Well, honey, sure, I'll help you!"

Here's how much I knew about co-writing: The first time he sent me an idea he had, he had about two lines. Before I turned around, I had finished it! I didn't plan to finish it; it just started coming! I called him back and said, "I got it!"

He said, "Well, I like it!"

It finally dawned on me that you're supposed to grab a verse and let the other person grab a verse, and all that. I just didn't know any better.

Scotty and I were writing over the phone. On my first in-person co-write session, I went to Nashville with my little tablet and pencil, and sat down with Daryl Williams and John Darin Rowsey. Well, we talked about the first hour and a half, just having a big time, before we really got started.

Daryl had written with John that morning, and he was supposed to leave. I was supposed to write with John in the afternoon. When Daryl got ready to go, he said that he would have loved to stay, but that he had promised his kids he'd take them somewhere. Well, about twenty minutes passed, and he came back in, and said, "I told my kids I couldn't do it!" (Only a songwriter would do that!)

So here I am, first time—maiden voyage—in the room with people, where the pressure's on. I thought, "Oh, nothing will come!"

But Daryl said, "I got this little chorus"—

It ain't gonna worry me long...

We finished it in no time, and we had so much fun. You could tell the kind—it was anything but high church. Someone came up with a word, and we said, "No, that's too high for this—this is low church, and that won't work!"

When we got through, Daryl sat down at the piano, and we worked out the arrangement and sang trio style. At the time, both Daryl and John were singing full-time with mixed groups. I was no longer singing with my family. I remember saying to Daryl and John, "You mean those girls you sing with actually take money to get to do this?" The work tape could have been on the radio, it was so good! The Talleys cut "It Ain't Gonna Worry Me Long" from that work tape.

I was thinking, "I'm a co-writer. I'm going to love it. It's all going to be just like this." Turn out something great, have a big ol' time, go home, get it cut.

I can't say every session's been that much fun, but I have found my level with a few writers. That's been a great blessing for me to do. I still love it when it's just the Lord and me. But it's really fun to co-write; it stretches you.

Joseph Habedank and I had been trying to get together for a long time to write a song. But I work, and he's gone a lot, so it hadn't worked out. One year, I saw the Perrys at Songfest (a huge three-day event which Frank Arnold brings to Jackson, Tennessee every year).

Joseph said, "It's so hard for us to get together! Maybe we could just write by email. Actually, I do have an idea."

I said, "What's the idea?"

"Footprints on the Water."

"Yes, I think you *do* have an idea!" You know how someone's face lights up when they're excited; his eyes were twinkling!

I had almost the whole lyric done before I got back to my house. My idea was, "You know, we're going to make this a different story. I'm going to make this from the vantage point of another boat full of fishermen: 'What am I seeing? Am I seeing what I think I'm seeing?'"

They realize they were being storm-tossed. And then in the moonlight they see this figure. Who is that?

Two days later, Joseph sends me an mp3. He doesn't play an instrument. So he sings you his melody, with his finger popping. And that child is full of rhythm!

He got Matthew Holt to play the piano on the demo. They had a hot track on that demo, and Gold City cut it.

Before Joseph got married, I teased him, saying, "After you get married, you're going to be like Scotty—you're not going to turn these things around in three days, like you've been doin'!"

"Oh, yes, I will!"

"Oh, no, you won't, you won't! Have you not read that excuse in the Bible about the man that said, 'I have married a wife, therefore I could not come'—have you not read that Bible excuse?"

He finished "Footprints" in two days! Well, he might not be that quick anymore, but we have kept writing. We wrote "I'm a Brand New Man"; the Kingdom Heirs cut it in 2011, on *We Will Stand Our Ground*. I wanted to do a lyric about Zacchaeus that wasn't about a "wee little man," but about what a low-down skunk he was before he got saved. I wanted to contrast that with what a huge difference it is when you become brand new. I sent the full lyrics to Joseph, and the whole rockin' melody and groove are his.

Another song we've written together is "A Cross Became My Saving Grace." It was my lyric and my idea, and he put a beautiful tune to it. Wilburn & Wilburn cut that on their major-label debut project in 2011.

"God Did it All" starts with Creation; the second verse is about the Cross. I am so tired of the ignorance of big bang theories and folks who deny what God has done. As Genesis says, God made the earth in six days. (I tell people there *will* be a big bang, but it will be when God dissolves the present heavens and earth and makes new ones!)

One day, I went over to Rusty Golden's house to write. I sent several lyrics ahead of time, and he had done something with just about all of them. He figured we'd work on some of those. But I had the brand new lyric to "God Did it All"; he'd never seen it.

I had the tune to the chorus and loved it, but I wasn't liking what I had for the tune of the verses. I realized it needed the Golden touch! For some reason—God—I just set it up on his piano music stand.

He got to reading those words and just began to play this gorgeous melody. When he got to the chorus, he wasn't sure where to go. I did something I never do—I walked over to the piano and played him what I had. It fit *perfectly*. We didn't change a word or a note from that point.

Rusty and I *never* write that way. It was just one of those times God showed up in a special way and took over a writing session. You can always feel His inspiration, but sometimes, you just feel His *presence*.

We got a *perfect* demo from Tim Parton and Terry Franklin, and we couldn't wait to pitch it to the Booth Brothers. Rick Shelton at Daywind sent it to Michael Booth on the same day that Rusty sent it to Ronnie Booth. They *both* put it on hold, and they cut it in 2010 on *Declaration*.

All my career long, even though I've written a lot of big ballads, my favorite kind to write is the up-tempo, scalding quartet song. My co-writers are stretching me more into power ballad country. With the possible exception of Marty Funderburk, there's just no one better at it than Rusty.

I have written two songs with Mosie Lister! I still cannot believe it.

Steve Mauldin got us together because Mosie had never done any co-writing. Probably, of everyone writing today, I'm the only one that's doing the old-time style that he would like. And I emailed him—he does email!—and he's kind of a taciturn gentleman. He doesn't have a lot to say. He sent me a lyric; it was called "The Amen Corner." It was about a guy walking into a church and asking, "Y'all got an amen corner in here? That's where I want to sit!"

We wrote that one and another one. Through the process, I was calling him Mr. Mosie because I thought, "I can't say Mosie! That would be like walking up to Dad Speer and saying, 'Hey, George! How 'ya doin?'"

He wrote me back and said, "If you call me Mr. Mosie, I don't answer. You gotta call me Mosie."

And I'm thinking, "I don't think I can!" But I got to where I could.

I still can't believe that I've written with him. And when we both were in the same songwriters' showcase at the 2009 National Quartet Convention, I'm goin', "Lord, how did you bless an ole Arkansas girl to that extent!"

Writing with Jerry Salley is like watching two people who have learned to tango beautifully. He's just gold to write with, and he's a good, good man. If you can't write with Jerry, you can't write with anyone—if you've got something in you, he'll get it out!

He is easy-going; I've never had to sit and write with someone who is temperamental. That would just devastate me; that would make me close up my little petals, and I would be afraid to say anything. I love him, just like a little brother.

I met him through Rusty Golden. I stopped by Rusty's house one day to drop off a couple of CDs, before driving over to Daywind. Rusty, Jerry, and Jim McBride were sitting in a room, writing. When I saw them, I thought, "Oh, I wish I didn't have to leave, I wish I didn't have to leave!"

I had met Jerry once before, but we visited that day. When I left, he said, "We're going to have to write sometime."

One day, I had an idea which I thought would make a great song. I decided to put out a little fleece. I emailed it out to several of my writer friends, and I said, "Wouldn't this make a good song?"

Jerry Salley wrote me back and said, "I got a chorus! I got a chorus!"

He had some lyrics—the title was going to be "Jesus Will"— and I sat down and put a tune to that chorus. Well, we set us up a session and finished it. It's a pretty thing, kind of Country Gospel. Rick Shelton sent it to Jonathan Wilburn, who cut it on Wilburn & Wilburn's mainline debut project.

I love to write with Scotty Inman, Rebecca Peck, Jerry Salley, Rusty Golden, Joseph Habedank, John Lemonis, Kyla Rowland, Dustin Sweatman, Ernie Haase, and so many others. But it is something real special when it's just you and the Lord.

There is a lot of pressure when you're co-writing in the room with somebody, and you know the Daywind people are going to shut the building down at 5:00. If you have everything done but the last half of the second verse, you do have the temptation, "Let's hurry up and get this one done, and get the work tape turned in!" But you have to be patient; a song takes as long as it takes. No one is looking for a good song...they're looking for a great song.

The Lord definitely led me to co-writing. I was a bit slow to start because I didn't think I would like it. In the old days, I turned in about twenty songs per year. That has drastically changed now. Not only do I turn in more songs that I write with others, but bouncing ideas off of other people gives me more ideas, so I turn in more that are just mine. So, like always, God knew best!

19

Roger Bennett was born in 1959; when I met him, it was probably early 1982. It was not long before he got married. He was from Strawberry, Arkansas, and his wife, Debbie, was from West Memphis, Arkansas. I was an Arkansan, also, and even lived in West Memphis. They went to a Baptist College in Walnut Ridge, which was near Blytheville.

As Roger and I got to be better friends, even though I was older than he was, there were groups in northeast Arkansas who we were both familiar with. Of course, they were younger when I heard them, but they were still singing when Roger started going to their concerts. So we had that in common.

Roger was close friends with Kirk Talley at the time. I met Kirk first because I was pitching songs to him. But the minute I met Roger, even with the age difference, there was an instant bonding. In some ways, I almost felt like he was my spiritual son; I had maternal pride in him. He was just a kid when I met him! But he was an amazing piano player.

Over the years, I watched him grow into a great husband, great dad, and hugely respected artist in his profession. He was still just as funny as ever. I became so proud of the man he grew into as he matured.

We had the same kind of offbeat humor. We would just look at each other and know exactly what the other one was going to say! He lived to try to get me, to hook me in with something ridiculous, make me think it was true, and get me going for a couple of minutes.

He was so good at it, and he was such a great actor. He could make real tears in this little game he liked to play. Sometimes, for a couple of minutes, he could get me on board.

Roger called me Dottie, as in Dottie Rambo. I called him Hovie, as in Hovie Lister. When email came along, he would greet me as Dottie, and he would sign his emails as Hovie! In fact, when I hear from Debbie, I still respond as "Dottie."

I also called him Roger Darlin'; the name on his birth certificate might have been Roger Douglas, but everyone knew his real name was Roger Darlin'!

Kirk Talley opened the door to the Cathedrals for me. But if I had to give anybody the most credit for the success of my writing career, it would be Roger Douglas Bennett. He always loved my writing, and if anyone asked him his favorite writer, he would say, "Dianne Wilkinson's my favorite."

He would get those homemade tapes from me. He would take them to George and Glen. They would listen, and he would tell them how he thought it could work. Those men would record my songs from those pitiful work tapes, and they did that for two decades. He kept my songs before those men as long as they were working as a quartet.

Then, he was the one screening songs for Legacy Five. From the moment he took over the screening of the music for the Cathedrals, until he was too weak and sick to continue screening the songs, he kept my songs out in front of those quartets.

I had always been known as the Cathedrals' songwriter, so when they retired, I wondered if my run was over. But when Roger Bennett and Scott Fowler founded Legacy Five, I had two on their first project, so it was almost like we didn't miss a beat. One of them was "Travelin' Shoes," a flying grassy track, and the other was "Salvation Is the Miracle."

Legacy Five did a showcase at Quartet Convention the year the Cathedrals retired. They were emotionally drained and physically exhausted from the schedule they kept up, and they knew how bad things were with Glen. And they were the most ballyhooed upcoming quartet ever because everybody knew that they were the next configuration of the Cathedrals. You can imagine how hard it was for them to walk out there; the pressure just had to be amazing. But they did a spectacular job.

I always dreaded for Roger to recognize me from the stage because I never knew what he was going to do. Now with the Cathedrals, George Younce always recognized me and had me stand; he was so gracious with what he said. All of my boys do that; Gerald Wolfe is particularly eloquent and so sweet about all he says. But when Roger had Legacy Five, and he was going to emcee, I was thinking, "Oh, please, God, 'cause we don't know what he's going to say!"

One night, Gail and I went to see them in Florence, Alabama. They hadn't been together very long. Gail loved Roger, too, because she was my friend all the way through and was just as close to him as I was.

That night, we got to town early. The concert was in a converted movie theater, right in downtown Florence, and we had a little time to kill. So we walked around the corner of that block, and there was a dress shop, with the shades down almost to the bottom of the door.

But we could see the light was on. I bent down and looked, and I could see there was still a lady in there, probably trying to close. Well, we knocked on the door, and we persuaded her to let us in to look around!

My eye fell on a rhinestone spider pin. It was just as big as a saucer. It is dimensional; its legs don't lay flat against your suit or jacket—they curve outward. Its body is a huge single block of a rhinestone. You wear it with something black and elegant, and your eyes just go to it!

I've worn this to Quartet Convention since, and it's really kind of legendary, since it's such an unusual piece of jewelry. Everywhere I've ever worn it, I've had people offer me money for it.

Anyway, I bought it and put it on because one of the things Roger loved the most about me was all that flash. When we would come in, he'd say, "Oh, put your sunglasses on, here she comes! She's going to blind you! There are going to be so many sequins you'll lose your eyesight! Here she comes! Here she comes!"

Well, he loved all that—the sequins, red fingernails, high-heel shoes, red hot cars, and big hair! When I replaced my Cadillac Coup deVille Bauritz with a pearly white car, he said, "Dottie, I miss the red car! I miss the red one! You're supposed to have a red car, not a white one."

So that night, I said, "Gail, I'm going to put this pin on; Roger will like that; he'll think it's cool." So I did! So when he recognized me that night, he had me stand. He said who I was, mentioned a lot of the songs, and said all of the right things.

And when I thought we were going to be okay, he said, "And y'all know what else? She's *riiiiiich*! Look at all them diamonds on her! She's so rich! She's written enough songs, there ain't no tellin' how much money she's got in the bank!"

When I finally got with him, I said, "You're going to get me killed! They're going to follow me to the car and mug me! And besides all that, it's a lie. I suspect there are no rich Gospel songwriters. You know it's a lie! Why do you say that?"

He said, "I don't know, Dianne, it just comes out. I can't help myself."

That is just one little story. There are so many!

I loved him with the same kind of love that I have for my only sibling, my preacher brother. It's almost like Roger was the baby brother Jim and I never had, but he got mixed up at birth and wound up in someone else's home! That's how I felt about that! He was the first one I looked for at Quartet Convention and the last one I hugged when I left.

And then, of course, his children came. They were like grandbabies to me, and I love them. I love Debbie, still to this day. She was the perfect wife for Roger. They fell in love with each other, and they never saw anyone else for the rest of their lives. She came to understand so well that the vows mean "for better or worse, in sickness and in health."

Roger battled chronic lymphoma in the 1990s, and he was in remission for a long time.

Roger had been friends with Tim and knew what we went through. The irony of our lives together was that Debbie had to go through the same thing, but much longer. With Tim and me, it was months, with them it was more like ten years.

We were at the Quartet Convention in 2005 or 2006 when I found out that it had turned into acute leukemia. Roger was at the edge of the stage, and he called me over. I said, "Roger, honey, what is it?"

He said, "I've got something to tell you. I just got back from Texas, and it has morphed into acute leukemia."

I thought my knees would not hold me up. I didn't even try to hide how bad it hurt.

I said, "Oh, honey, we gotta double-time the prayer now. What's the plan?"

He said, "Well, they're talking about bone marrow transplants and that kind of thing."

If you can believe this, in no time after that, he got on that stage, and turned into *Roger Bennett*. He just turned it on.

As things got bad, he said to me, "Listen, Dottie. I know I'm a sick man, but we're not going to act like I'm a sick man. Our relationship's going to be like it's always been. Don't you get serious on me. Don't you get scared or pitiful on me. We're going to keep it light."

I said, "Honey, I'll do the best I can."

And I did. I did the best I could. There were a few times when my email back to him had to show what I was feeling more than I meant for it to. He didn't want anything about our relationship to change. And I know now, that's how everybody feels. They don't want their whole life to become, "I'm a sick person who's probably going to die. That's all anybody knows about me."

Roger spent the final months of his life at M.D. Anderson in Texas. Even at his worst, people would come in to talk to him, to get encouragement from *him*.

He educated a lot of people out there about Southern Gospel music. They asked what he did for a living, and he would explain what separates our music from other kinds of music. Of course, he'd been in it long enough to do that really well.

That's really the only time he talked much about what he did for a living. He never brought it up and talked about it, when he certainly could have. He was absolutely a star in our business, but that was not the Roger who was in Texas, unless someone asked him about it. He just testified of the goodness and the grace of God.

He was always funny; he always kept his wit. Debbie said he bore all this tremendous burden with such grace. His attitude was, "I'll get my healing. It may not be here, but I'll get it."

If all you knew about Roger was how funny he was, you might not think there was depth of character there. You have to be really, really smart to be that funny. But underneath all the fun was a deep and solidly anchored faith in God that never left Roger.

No one in the world could have taken care of Roger Darlin' like Debbie did. She was so wise, and she was funny, too. She tried to keep their life as normal as she could, even in his last days at M.D. Anderson. She said, "Dianne, I'm so glad you couldn't see him; he was so frail."

How hard it must have been for her! I know something about that. One day she walked into his room and said, "Well, I want to tell you something. I've looked up and down all the floors in this joint, and there ain't nobody in here as good-looking as you, period. You are the best-looking thing I've ever seen!"

When people talk about their female heroes—the President's wife, lady authors, and the like—my female hero is Debbie Bennett. She never, ever looked like she was tired. She never said, "I can't go another a mile. I can't move to M.D. Anderson and leave my kids, can't do it, can't do it." When it was Christmas time at that little apartment at M.D. Anderson, the first thing she'd do was put up a tree, to make it home. She was Debbie Darlin', like Roger was Roger Darlin'. She is like a daughter to me still.

I remember the morning Scott called me and said, "I have something bad to tell you." I knew he was going to tell me that Roger had died.

I had never gotten any satisfaction that God was going to heal Roger here. When I realized how he was suffering, I began to pray, "Lord, would You just have mercy, and shorten these days for the elect's sake, and take him home?"

I told Scott, "It breaks my heart, but I wouldn't have had him another day, the way he was." He had just gone down so fast.

Debbie knew exactly how to plan the perfect funeral for her husband. Roger's funeral was so perfect and tasteful. It reflected all that was Roger, humor included. She couldn't have planned it better; it was just wonderful. I was so glad to get to go.

One of the coordinators at M.D. Anderson, who had become close to Roger and Debbie, actually spoke at his funeral. She said that at M.D. Anderson, Roger Bennett will never be forgotten. He made such an impact on that huge organization. He was just that kind of person.

Of course, the funeral was closed-casket; it had to be. My last memories of seeing him were when he was ill. But I don't think of Roger how he looked at the end; I think of Roger before he got so sick, when he was tall, filled out, and handsome, with that pretty hair and those twinklin', mischievous eyes!

Debbie included some songs Roger loved. None of us may have known that they were some of his favorites, but nobody knows you like your wife does. She had lots of video footage of the family when they were out on vacation. You saw them out in the snow with their warm hats on; that was a side of Roger I didn't get to see much. He was very much a family man, and that all came out in his funeral.

Roger and I had talked once about which one of us might die first; we both had health problems. He looked at me and said, "Dottie, don't you wear a plain black dress to my funeral, if I go first. I want you to wear sequins to my funeral, so I'll know it's you when you pass by."

So when the time came, I wore a black skirt, and I also wore a sequined top. If anyone thought I was overdressed, they didn't know the relationship that Roger and I had.

When I spoke to Debbie at the funeral, she said, "You dressed for Roger Darlin' today, didn't you?"

And I said, "Yes."

We *both* knew that even though his name was Roger Douglas Bennett, his real middle name was Darlin'.

One day, I picked up my Singing News. Danny Jones' column is the first thing you read, right in the front. The story is legendary now; Roger had written something and told Danny to put it in the Singing News after he went Home to Glory. It was a message to some of his friends.

Of course, he singled out Mark Trammell, Darrell Stewart, Scott Fowler, and Rodney Griffin. He had my name in there; he had a message for me from beyond the grave.

He said: "Thank you for the songs, and for letting me have the opportunity of calling you a songwriting colleague. Keep writing, and by all means, make sure you send all of your really good songs to Legacy Five. That's L-E-G-A-C-Y F-I-V-E. Do you need the address? Remember: Legacy Five."

I can't tell you the emotion I felt from that, but that shows you how close we were.

Roger was unique among all the friends I've had in my life; I never will stop missing him. To this day, the way I describe that personal loss is: There's a Roger-shaped hole in my heart that nobody else can fill.

20

My first Gold City cut was "I'm Goin' Home Someday," in the early 1980s. We were well into the '90s before I got my next two, "I've Passed Over into Canaanland" and "Longing for Beulah Land."

When they cut "He Said" in 1999, it was my first #1 hit since "Boundless Love." Everybody thinks I've had a million #1 hits, but I haven't; several of my Cathedrals singles came just short of #1. There were three major radio charts at the time, and it was #1 two months running in all three of those! That rarely happens these days!

I saw a statistic that in the whole decade of the 2000s, "He Said" was #2 in radio airplay for the whole decade. It was the biggest non-Cathedrals hit I ever had.

Niles Borop had me re-write the second verse. I had it a lot more in-your-face, and Niles was afraid it would hurt its chances of getting cut! So I re-wrote it; I'm not sure I would have done that now. He hadn't known me long enough then to know how much I could get away with!

When Gold City was picking songs for their *Are You Ready?* album, they cut three of mine—"Keep Me on the Wheel," "Saved," and "Since Jesus Touched Me."

Shortly before they went into the studio, Jonathan Wilburn came up to me at the Southern Gospel Music Association awards dinner. We were talking about his vision for "Keep Me on the Wheel." I told him, "You know, I hear it like the Fairfield Four, those old black gentlemen in overalls."

He said, "Oh, I hear Elvis; I hear Elvis."

Mark Trammell did the arrangement. It remains one of my top three favorite cuts of all time. It never went to radio.

When I wrote "Saved," my whole point was describing to a lost person who had never even heard about our faith what it means to be saved. Christians know what that means, but how would you describe what it's like?

I wanted to make it as strong as I could to explain to someone who has no clue what salvation is like.

When I sent Mark my work tape, after I sang it to him on the phone, it was my idea to include the little riff off of the old hymn "Saved, Saved." It fits perfectly with the meter of that song, and he kept that in the final version.

Tim Riley told me once that when they sang in those old-time Baptist churches, that's the song that would get the preachers to shouting!

One time, Arthur Rice was producing a record for a young lady who had been Miss Tennessee and had used a Gospel song for her talent performance. She asked me for songs; I sent her some, and she cut five of them! She cut "Saved"; her version almost had a lilting quality. It wasn't the power punch doctrinal thing Gold City had, but it was beautiful in its own way.

So when I sent the song to Karen Peck, I sent her this version. I didn't even think about telling her that it had been recorded before because it sounded so different! (Also, Gold City never sent it to the radio!)

Well, Karen loved it, and she wanted it for Susan. But that's when that little old quartet encyclopedia, Devin McGlamery, was singing with her. He said, "I remember that song! Gold City cut that song!"

Karen said, "You mean, it's been recorded before?"

He said, "Oh, yeah, but it's real different!"

Well, when I saw her, we got to laughing about it. I said, "Karen, I am so sorry." I didn't withhold it from her on purpose—I didn't even make the connection!

She said, "Oh, we'd 'a done it anyway! It is so different. We didn't remember it, but he did!" Those little old quartet boys, they know everything that's ever been cut by their favorite groups.

When Mark Trammell left Gold City, I wasn't sure if I'd ever get another cut then, because he was screening songs for them, and

I didn't know Danny Riley that well. When it got to the place where Danny had the quartet, the first thing he did was call over and say, "Send me everything you got!"

I thought, "Oh, but that's good news!"

The next thing I knew, they cut "That Little Baby"! They didn't even treat it like a Christmas song. They sent it right on to the radio, and I think it reached #2.

The Ruppes also recorded it on a Christmas album. Then I had the great blessing of getting it in Mike Speck's Christmas book, which is still the all-time biggest-selling choral book for Christmas. It's kind of a perennial thing now for church choirs since they've all sung it for so long.

At the 2009 Quartet Convention, I was just Cinderella. What can I say? I was in the top five nominees for writer in the Singing News Fan Awards and had three of the top ten songs —"What Salvation's Done for Me," "Jesus Made a Believer out of Me," and "Old White Flag."

At the awards ceremony, I was sitting in the artist circle with Jerry Salley. Rusty Golden's and my song, "What Salvation's Done For Me," won. I still remember thinking, "How do you react? How can you stand much of this? It's so good, how can you stand it?"

Rusty wasn't able to attend, so I spoke for both of us. I hadn't been on that stage with a winning song since 1995. It felt good to be back, and I was so happy it was a Booth Brothers song.

There's a reason why the fans love them so—they are wonderful young men.

I still think of the Collingsworth children as the age they were when they graciously invited me to come up and be a guest at the taping of their 2007 *Your Ticket to Music Hall* DVD, where they sang my song, "He Already Sees." A few years can make a huge difference in a teenager. Boom, they're grown!

I love the whole family, but Phil Sr. ... what can you say about him? Mr. Personality! His personality is just infectious!

Here's how gracious they are: When they cut their most recent album, they sent out an email to all the writers whose songs they had on hold. They thanked everyone for sending songs, and then they listed the ones they choose. That lets you know you can start pitching the ones that didn't get cut to somebody else. They are a class act of how to do business.

When Mark Trammell put his quartet together, I told someone, "All the big quartets better watch it, 'cause Mark has come to play! He's in the game! He's got it! And he's got the quartet. They've got the sound."

They sound more like the Cathedrals than *anyone* else. The blend, and Mark's baritone, just call them up. And Pat Barker can sound just like George Younce when he wants to!

The first time I ever heard Pat do George, they were at my house on a Saturday afternoon and evening. (For some reason, they had Saturday off.) They came back for dinner on Sunday because they were at a church close by.

I have a huge collection of old quartet records. The boys were lying on the floor, close to the turntable, listening to old Cathedral records. On every single song, Pat was singing along. If I had shut my eyes, I would've thought it was George!

He was doing George, not to prove he could do George, but his mind and heart were going back to the Cathedrals. That's the way it was coming out! I said, "Pat, you can do George to a T!"

He said, "You know, I don't plan it, but he's my hero, and sometimes it just comes out."

I was somewhat familiar with Pat, but I didn't know what Mark had till I began to hear him with them. Pat is such a precious man; he's a Bible student and a Godly young man, exactly who needs to be travelin' with a Baptist preacher. He just became one of my boys right away.

After a few years off the road, Jonathan Wilburn started Wilburn & Wilburn with his son, Jordan, in 2011. He cut five of my songs on their major-label debut!

His fans didn't even know what he can do. They know the "He Said" Jonathan, the "Keep Me on the Wheel" Jonathan, and the "I'm Not Givin' Up" Jonathan. But they didn't know he could sing bluegrass as well as anybody in the world. He cut one that's full-out bluegrass, "You'll Still Be There." It is grass to the bone, and he is wearing it out!

His son Jordan is amazing, too.

I thought, "Wait 'till they hear Jonathan do that grass!" It's kind of bluesy grass; it's not "Old White Flag" grass.

I said, "Jonathan, tell me the truth—did you know old Di could write grass like that?"

And he said, "I didn't, I didn't. I mighta known, but I didn't!"

I said, "Well I didn't know you could sing grass like that, either! I might have known, but I didn't!" This record is diverse— but all within the Southern Gospel genre. It's wonderful, and I know God is going to use Wilburn & Wilburn in a mighty way.

I already mentioned how Ernie Haase & Signature Sound cut "Pray for Me" and "This Old Place" on their breakout project, *Ernie Haase & Signature Sound*, in 2005. In 2010, they recorded *A Tribute to the Cathedral Quartet*, a CD and DVD, and brought back "We Shall See Jesus" and "Boundless Love." They protected the feel of the songs from what the Cathedrals had, but they still put their own style on them.

So many of the others who did Cathedrals songs avoided "We Shall See Jesus," because it was Glen's song. But Devin McGlamery just stepped up there—twenty-six years old!—and sang his heart out. I could almost see Glen just clapping and saying, "Bravo for Devin," because he did such a great job.

To be invited to the DVD taping—and to be surrounded by Debbie Bennett, Van Payne, Van's children and grandchildren, and George's children—was very, very emotional for me. It was classy, and a perfect honor to the most beloved quartet we've ever had.

21

I have written around 700 songs, not counting the early ones that were lost. With as long as I've been writing, that's not a huge body of work. Before I started co-writing, I would write about twenty a year. I have turned in fifty or more per year since I started co-writing.

Depending on how long the Lord leaves me here, and how long He keeps giving me songs, I don't know if I'll break a thousand. That's totally up to Him!

Rick Shelton, my publisher at Daywind, tells me that my songs have a cut rate of about 65%-70%; that's a blessing because that's pretty high. That means there are 30%-35% that people are probably never going to hear. I think of it this way: I learned that some of the songs I wrote when my husband was alive were only going to be sung by him.

Sometimes the songs God gives are just for me at a certain time in my life. I think that they all have value, but I don't know that they all have commercial value. I do like to think that someday a bunch of them will still get cut.

Secular music, like Country music, has waves of what's popular. But the neat thing about our music is that a great Southern Gospel song was great in 1980, great in 1990, and it's still great! Somebody can cut a new track, with a different twist, and it's brand new again because our subject matter doesn't change.

I've been a church musician since twelve years old. It really helps to understand harmony, chords, and chord progressions, and to be able to execute those chords when you put your song together. If you don't play any instruments, you can hear what you want in your head, but it would be hard to tell the musicians making the demo exactly what you want.

Sometimes I write songs a bit too hard for me to play! They'll take me places where I can't find the chord quite so well. That's when I trust Tim Parton, who records the tracks for my song demos, and tell him what I want. I'll say, "You play it just like I did, only better!" He always knows what I mean by that.

It also helps to be a poet who understands meter and how to put the lyric together in such a way that you catch your idea but still keep your rhyme and rhythm.

There are a lot of people who want to write more than anything, and they just don't have that gift. That is so sad! They're living their lives in frustration because they're probably overlooking the gifts they do have.

Songwriting skills can be honed, especially if you start with an ear for it. When you have a love for Southern Gospel music, you listen and pay attention. You analyze the songs you love, asking, "What do I love about that song? Well, I really like the way the melody is. I love the way the chords go together. I love the way the tune moves."

You might not know if it's a diminished or augmented chord, but you can say, "I love the place where it hits that odd chord." When you do that, you can learn songwriting. But I still believe God gives you the gift and calls you to use it.

There's just something special when you're in tune with the Lord and a song just comes out of the blue. I think those are the dearest ones to me; it's hard to explain what it feels like.

That happens to me a lot in the car, when I'm alone and not distracted. I have written so many songs in the car—including "Turn Your Back" (Cathedrals), "There is a Haven" (Cathedrals), "This Old Place" (Ernie Haase & Signature Sound), "Strike Up the Band" (Legacy Five), and "Lord, I Always Know That I Can Count on You" (Kingdom Heirs).

Not every song reveals His presence in a chilling way. But still, you know it's God. You know He's given you something that He meant for you to have. I may not be thinking about writing, but here it comes!

I recently decided—reluctantly—to get a laptop computer for co-writing sessions. Behind the piano at Daywind, there used to be a music stand. There is now a stand just right to hold a laptop. My other co-writers have laptops, so I was like the dinosaur!

I would never write on a laptop when writing by myself. But when co-writers want to change something, it's a whole lot different—more to negotiate. I wind up with all these cross-outs. Somebody will say, "You know what, it's not workin'; let's just scratch this and start all over." That doesn't really happen to me when I'm writing by myself!

I loved for one of us to have the laptop, so we could put our work version on a disc, and I could leave there with it. But I liked being the one with the tablet and pencil—and some of my writer friends still like for me to be the one with the tablet and pencil. They can go back and say, "Now what did you have on that page a while ago? I already deleted that."

But when I write by myself, I have a regular legal pad tablet and a good writing ballpoint pen. I sit, and I start.

I can't explain it. Even if I begin an idea in the car, something about sitting in the chair, getting the tablet in my lap and the pen in my hand, and praying that the Lord will guide it, just makes my pen move. I can't explain why; it just happens.

And I have to have perfect quiet. Of course, I live by myself. I don't want anything on—no TV, no racket, perfect quiet. If I can get in that setting, pray over it, and develop my thought, it usually doesn't take all that long to get what I want to get done.

Drafting lyrics on tablets is why I was able to give Glen Payne the original lyric to "We Shall See Jesus" in 1994. I was also able to give Clayton Inman the original tablet pages to "Old White Flag" at a songwriters' showcase. I also sent Arthur Rice the original tablet pages for "When You Look at Me." Warts and all, it's what you want to give them. You don't want to clean it up. That would take all the beauty out of it. I still save the original lyrics; I have a boatload of paper in my cabinets.

It seems like the Devil does everything he can to distract us from writing. For me, it's through technology.

I paid some serious money for a printer in 2010. The main thing I use it for is to print off lyrics so I can turn in my songs. Nothing I could do would get this thing to print right. Finally my niece Rachel came, and we thought she had it fixed.

I told her, "As soon as you walk out this door, it won't print the very next page. It won't." Nothing would work, so I had to buy a new printer.

It's like the Devil tries to do everything he can to cripple the songwriter, to keep you from getting it done. He'll mess up your computer. He'll fix it where you can't get your mp3s in. He'll do something.

My writer friends and I talk about it all the time. We decide it's an honor if he's doing that because that means he's scared of us! He wouldn't be bothering somebody if they weren't writing the truth. So we count it an honor!

After I finish a song, the next step is preparing a work tape. A work tape is different than a finished demo; I am just playing the piano and singing the melody. Terry Franklin does the vocals on my finished demos, and Tim Parton often does the tracks. I tell them exactly what I want them to do—if I want the song to feel a certain way, or have an echo. I have the transpositions, the arrangement, and the big ending in mind, so the demo comes out like I want it. Many times, groups think they can't improve on that demo, so I wind up getting just what was in my head!

After years of sinus problems, my voice is nothing like it used to be. I can't quite execute some of the high notes, so I'll play the note at the end and say, "This is where I think the end note ought to go, right here."

Tim and Terry know my style so well that they instinctively know what I want on a certain kind of song. This is such a great blessing for me because when I turn one in that might sound ragged vocally, nobody will ever know when they get back what they've done.

Other than the three on the Eddie Crook demos, all of my Cathedrals cuts came from work tapes. For "We Shall See Jesus," I sent the only copy I had because I knew that I would still be able to sing it. I wouldn't forget it.

Roger couldn't believe it when I got hooked up with Niles Borop, and he would actually get a CD with Terry Franklin singing all the parts—a for-real demo. He would say, "They're all great, but I still want your work tape. I still want you singin'."

And he kept them! He told me once—this is hard for me to say without crying—"When I get to missin' you, Dottie, I play those tapes, and ride along in the car and listen to you talk, and laugh again at all you're tellin' me."

"Nobody gives instructions like you do, Di," he would say. "Always do that." He wanted what was in my head. Now he might embellish or even change it, but he wanted what I was hearing, and he wanted to hear my vocal, some little touch I put on it.

Rick Shelton told me that often other writers just send something in and figure it will come out okay. But I am too obsessive-compulsive for that! I have an arrangement in my head, and I know exactly what I'm looking for. I don't leave it to chance!

I'll say, "Tim, I want quartet piano out front, maybe a little bass sound, maybe a little drum, nothin' else." I've been working long enough with him now that I don't have to go into as much detail; sometimes I say, "Tim, this one sounds like a hymn, and I want all those marvelous hymn sounds that you do, and you know what I mean."

Some of my quartet boys still want my work tapes. Ernie Haase wants them. He loves that quartet-style piano; he'll say, "I don't care if you send the other one or not; I want to hear you."

And I'm thinking, "You're a glutton for punishment, honey, that's what you are!"

Mark Trammell doesn't even need a work tape; he cut "Saved" after I pitched it on the telephone. He just hears the whole thing in his head!

My quartet boys all tease me, "Don't ever have to worry about what Dianne's hearin' because she's going to tell you!"

I say, "Well, it's my song, and it came from the Lord to me, and I want it to stay that way, and I stand a better chance of it this way! I mean, y'all may hear something in there you wanna use."

I'm legendary for doing that, but it serves me well! I just can't toss it off and say, "Here's a work tape, do whatever you think."

Once I send in a work tape, sometimes it takes a while to get a demo. If I were a rich woman—filthy rich like Oprah—I would put Tim Parton on retainer, and I would pay him enough that when mine came in, he would stop whatever he was doing and do them. That would be along with my personal chef, who could cook my Weight Watchers® food for me, and my personal trainer, who would keep me in a size twelve! I would have all that, and I would have both Tim Parton and Terry Franklin on retainer!

Songwriting seminars tell you to never send more than four songs at once to a group. MP3s over email is a nice thing, but occasionally my boys will still say, "Put everything you've got available on a disc and send it to me, so that we can play it on the bus, with all of us around the CD player listening."

They get the best of what I have available at the time; they hear them all. I have sent people a disc with twenty before, because they've asked me to. I've handpicked them, and it has paid off!

Oh, how I love to pitch songs! I have the reputation of being the most shameless song pitcher, especially face to face! It's in the personality; groups expect that and like it.

I love to write songs, and I love to pitch them. My publisher pitches to people I don't have a real personal relationship with, but I'll never let a publisher do all my pitching! It's worked well for me, especially to my pet groups, the ones with the long relationships.

I don't only pitch songs to full-time artists. I always send songs upon request to new groups and regional groups. When they ask for songs, if they don't specify, I ask, "Do you only want something that's never been cut, or would you take something that's been cut but never went to radio and was barely staged—still has a lot of life in it?"

The wise ones say, "Absolutely, send those to us."

What I want to tell them is, "If you take one of mine that's never been cut, it's probably made the rounds; maybe it's been on hold and hasn't been cut. It's probably not one of my strongest ones, or it still would not be cut because I have a high rate of cuts. Maybe it's just a good, good song, but it's not great!"

But some songs with greatness in them just die on the record. So you need to think about it! I have had some wonderful cuts from part-time and regional groups over the years.

22

In my part of northeast Arkansas, it was common for towns to have singing conventions every month. They would bring the latest Stamps-Baxter songbooks in and sing all those songs. Churches also had singing schools, with old gentlemen coming in to teach the shape notes.

Children don't grow up now learning music unless they're taking lessons. It's not happening in church, and it's not happening in school. So in my part of the country, unless a church has a real minister of music who's teaching people, choirs don't read music anymore. Even in pretty good-sized choirs now, almost everyone is singing the lead, with maybe some altos. You don't have basses and tenors—all the men are singing the melody, 'cause they don't read music! When choirs use tracks from choral books, the track has a pre-recorded choir. A smart sound man can kinda raise the vocals up in that track; it sounds like your choir's just doing great!

When I was a kid, people could actually read the parts to those Stamps-Baxter songs, and the whole place would ring with harmony. It's going away, and that's a tragic thing. I was blessed to grow up in that era; it contributed in a huge way to my writing style.

Sheet music has almost entirely vanished from our industry. I still get emails from people looking for sheet music. They have their own pianist or their own orchestra, and they want the music.

Many fabulous church musicians don't play by ear; they have to have the sheet music. They can play flawlessly with the music! Of course, if you have an orchestra, the music director needs the score.

I love to accompany people who sing; it's one of the things I love best in life. When you're playing for someone who is singing, you watch their mouth. You instinctively know when they're going to slow down for effect, and you stay with them. Tracks don't let you do that.

I wish sheet music was still available for individual songs at the artists' product tables, as it was years ago. But now the song has to be included in a compilation songbook or eventually become available as a digital download in order for the people to have the music. I don't have to write the music out to turn a song in to Daywind, so on almost all requests for sheet music, I have to say, "It's not available."

It's trendy among the bigger churches to love praise and worship music—to the point that if a Southern Gospel fan went to their church, it's almost like they'd have to be a closet fan.

I hate the idea that if you're the least bit intelligent, well-read, or well-educated, that you would like some other kind of music. We know that there are quartets where the tenor just squeals and squeals, and the bass man just growls and growls. If that's all they've heard, they might think that's all there is.

I will go to my grave saying that one man is responsible for changing a lot of that: Bill Gaither. He put the best of what we have on TV in a big way. I have friends in large mainline churches who love our music now, because they have watched the Homecoming videos. They say to me, "I didn't know there was that kind of music in the world!"

And I'll say, "Well, I was blessed to know that there was, because I got to go to singings when I was just a kid. I was blessed to be in a family where Gospel music was loved."

Mike Speck has brought our music into choral form without taking the pep or excitement out of it, making it mainstream music for the choirs in some of the biggest churches. So those two men deserve great credit for elevating Southern Gospel music into places where it would never have been before.

Back in the day, if a song was good enough, more than one group would cut it. There was probably more than one factor, but I think that the single biggest thing that stopped it in its tracks was the advent of the radio singles chart system. It got to be where if anybody ever sent a song to radio, that was it.

The two who benefited the most from everybody cutting their songs were Bill Gaither and Dottie Rambo. Everybody cut those songs! The one song I had then, "Behold the Lamb," was cut by the Songmasters, the Hoppers, Jerry and the Goffs, and even the Greenes.

Back in the old days, you'd send DJs a record. They played everything on it. The fans picked the hit by what they requested. Now, on the other hand, most of the time the powers-that-be, whoever they are, decide the single.

People know you by your singles. But, unless you buy the CD, you'll never know about "Keep Me On the Wheel," "When You Look at Me," or even "We Shall See Jesus." None of those went to radio!

There are others. One that grieves me is "Mountain of Grace." It was on Phillip Hughes' last record with the Kingsmen. It was a ballad, one of my favorite ballads that I've written in fifteen years. I think it's very strong, and I thought he sang it beautifully. I loved it.

Phillip thought that was the song they would single instead of "God Saw a Cross." But he left right after that, and they never even staged it. You never know how those things will go.

I knew "Mountain of Grace" was going to be a big, big song for somebody, and it could have been them. You get to where you say, "I'm going to wait a few years and pitch it again! That song should not die like that!" But somebody will find out that the Kingsmen cut it, and that will probably hurt its chances.

Another example was "I Found Mercy," one that Jerry Kelso and I wrote for the Kingsmen. Jeremy Peace, their tenor singer, sang lead on it, and it was sung very little.

When the Booth Brothers cut "God Did it All," Rusty Golden and I thought it was going to radio; it was not sent out as a single, but it did go to print as a choral music arrangement by Lari Goss and also by Brentwood-Benson.

So not only do people not always record the song again and again, sometimes one that you know has greatness in it might not reach its full potential initially. That's when you have to trust God. He's still in control of the songs.

23

As I said before, I have always had the whispering from the Lord, "Your end will be better than your beginning." From the very beginning, God just progressed my life along, at His pace. My beginnings weren't great, but God was with me every step of the way.

At various points, I thought, "Well, the writing has been great, but this is probably the end of the line." I sure thought that when the Cathedrals were winding down!

Then you think, "Well, I'm 50; how long to do you get to write after you get 50? Well, I'm 60; how long do you get to write...?" So many writers have a season of productivity and success, and then it winds down. But just when I think I've had a great run, God lets me keep on.

Partly because I have begun to co-write, I'm writing more songs now than I ever did. I have tried hard to be a faithful steward of the gift; God is growing my gift in my sunset years. It's a beautiful thing to watch.

At this stage in my life, for the first time, I had both the #1 and #2 songs on the Singing News charts, and the #2 went to #1 the next month. (These were "Peter, James and John" by Gold City, #1 on the March 2012 charts, and "Tell Me Why" by the Kingdom Heirs, #2 that month and #1 in April.) And I can't think of a time in my life when I've ever had so many songs on the chart!

It's just the most incredible and humbling thing that, after all these years, someone who started in her twenties can still sit down and turn out a song that will bless someone.

I could have arthritic hands and not be able to play anymore —not even well enough to play my work tapes for Terry Franklin and the track players to make the demos. That could happen, but it hasn't. God's still allowing me to do it at this age, and I'm so very thankful!

The older I get, the more I'm aware that I don't know how much time I have left.

I don't know if I'll always be able to put two words together. My prayer is that until I pass on, or until Jesus comes, He will still give the song and give me the mind to flesh it out and put it on paper. From the time He began with me, He has never pulled back for several years and given me nothing. It hasn't happened.

I have a burning desire to write—for as long as I'm able to write well. I've talked to a few people whom I trust and value and said, "When I can't do it anymore, pull me aside, and give me the word."

They're people who love me, and they say, "Oh, we don't think we could ever do that!"

But I say, "Don't let me be unaware; don't let me start turning out junk just because I want to keep doing it."

God still gives the ideas. I just know I will wake up one day and never think of a good one again. I'm hoping that when it happens, my co-writers will shine on me with favor and send me some of their ideas!

I'd like to keep writing till He comes. I'd really like to see the rapture! I want to cheat death! But I want to write what God has for me to write till I go.

If I never wrote another thing, and I was still here, that would grieve me. But I would be happy with what He gave me—because it was what was supposed to be given.

I want to keep writing the best I can write, craft it the best I can craft it, and give it the best I've got, as long as I can get it done. Writers like to think our best song is still in us.

I want to use what time I have left to get doctrinal truth and the Gospel message out on paper. Southern Gospel is the only genre doing this to that deep degree. I want to get the message out while there's still time. I know we're in the last days. I know there's not much time. So I feel an urgency.

I don't think songwriters will be able to quit writing songs in Heaven. I think we'll want to put down on Heavenly parchment what it looks like! We won't be saying, "We Shall See Jesus." We'll be saying, "I Have Seen Jesus!"

I want to write a song with David! "David, I know you like praise, and I know you dance, 'cause the Bible says so. Let's write an upbeat song up here!"

We won't be writing about sin and repentance. But we'll still be talking about everything Jesus did for us, and what a great God we have!

There *will* be music there!

I can't wait!

Appendix

Song Stories

A Love That Wouldn't Die
Integrity / Triumphant Quartet

After Clayton Inman left Won by One, he was going to start a trio with his son and a third singer. He has been my friend since my husband and I lived in West Memphis. He lived in Memphis with all his brothers, so I knew him well.

He wanted me to send him some songs, so I sent him a mixture. "A Love that Wouldn't Die" was on the disc.

Rather quickly after that happened, Jeff Stice, David Sutton, and Eric Bennett followed the call to Louise Mandrell and left the Kingdom Heirs. And as God would have it, they were in need of a lead singer and a baritone singer. They were already friends with

Clayton and Scotty, who lived right there in East Tennessee. So they put them in the quartet.

I sent Jeff some more songs. There was another one they liked, and I thought they were going to cut it. They hadn't said a word about "A Love That Wouldn't Die." But when the record came out, Jeff called me and said, "Oh, we cut 'A Love That Wouldn't Die,' and we just love it." I had no idea they were even interested in that song!

I said, "Who's singing lead?"

He said, "Clayton."

I loved the way they did the song. I learned something about Clayton—I learned what a range he has!

That was the first cut I had on Integrity/Triumphant. It was their very first recording, and it started something that's still going on.

It has since been recorded by Steve Ladd on his solo project. He really did a great job on it.

When I was writing it, the hymn "Oh Love That Wilt Not Let Me Go" was in the back of my mind. When the man was under conviction, the Lord just wouldn't let him rest! He wouldn't let him continue to be lost. He pursued him, and loved him, and wouldn't let him die!

A New Thing
Brian Free & Assurance

This was inspired on a day my brother was preaching out of Isaiah 43:19, "Behold, I will do a new thing." I got to pondering on how well that would work lyrically.

Most of the time when his sermon would direct me to a song, I'd start getting it on the way home. My church is about eight miles out from the main part of town, so it's a pretty good little clip to think. It started coming really rock-flavored.

Rick Shelton got Adam Kohout to do a full-band track. Their track was absolutely stupendous, one of the best I've ever heard. Terry Franklin's demo vocal is amazing, one of the best he's ever done. I was talking to him about how he had done it, and he said, "You know, when you get a track that great, you really have to sing up to that standard."

It sounded like Brian Free & Assurance. It didn't sound like the Kingdom Heirs, and it didn't sound like Legacy Five. I thought, "You know, if Brian doesn't take this, I'm probably stuck with it!" He did love it, and he did do it.

I had not had a cut with Brian since "Deep Water." (He has also done a couple of covers of "I'm Going Home Someday.")

Brian Free & Assurance lead singer Bill Shivers has told me that the crowd always loved it. I was a little worried what audiences would think; I thought, "This sounds like a rock band. What are they going to say?" But what I wanted audiences to do was listen to what the lyrics said in that song. If you've got one that has that hot a groove, you'd really better say something deep in the lyrics.

All in God's Own Time
Cathedral Quartet
See Chapter 11.

Arise
The Whisnants

My brother Jim preached one morning on the passage of Scripture where the Lord spoke to the little maid who had died. The song wasn't hard to write, at all. Of course, you know that you're going to talk about the Rapture, the whole point being arising.

When you sing it, you can feel it's a spiritual song, a shouter kind of song. It was Rick Shelton's idea to send it to the Whisnants. I had never had a Whisnants cut, but it's the same record as "King Jesus is Coming," so I got two!

It's the kind of song that would fit almost any vocal configuration; obviously, a mixed group did it great. I absolutely loved their cut!

As Good as I Can Be
Kingdom Heirs

This song is real close to me because it's real close to Steve French.

My little brother inspired it because he was a precocious little boy. He was never a mean little boy, but he was creative about having ideas that sounded good to him at the time, but turned out to be something that would get him a spanking! He was just curious, like, "Our neighbor's garage door sure looks real pretty white, but wouldn't it look nice with some green on it?"

My thought was, to people who think they can be good enough to make Heaven, there's only one way to be as good as you can be, and that's to be saved. So I wanted to play on words in it.

So, of course, I wrote the little boy being in trouble. When I wrote it and sent it to Steve, they were getting ready to cut, and he said, "I haven't found me one yet. I don't know that I'll have one on here."

I said, "Oh, honey, I think you ought to do my little boy song."

He said, "Little boy song?"

I said, "You know, the one about the little boy that got in trouble."

He had forgotten about it. He dug back through his CD. He called back and said, "Dianne, that song is me! I was that little bad boy!"

He was always a big kid, big for his age. Even if someone was older than he was, he'd just knock 'em out! He was bad to fight. Actually, there's a line in there about "grieved my mama's soul"— He said, "My Mama has looked at me before, and said, you grieeeeeeeeeeeeeeeeve me, Steve French!" So he was a trial to his mama when he was little bitty. And he can really sing it with some passion.

His voice can sound a lot like Ricky Skaggs. I love his solo voice even though he doesn't sing a feature often. My dear brother sings this one, too, and his line is "life just worked against me!"

Behold the Lamb
The Songmasters, The Hoppers, Dove Brothers, Jerry Goff
See Chapter 6.

Biblically Correct
Kingdom Heirs

Rusty Golden and I wrote this song in his living room in Hendersonville, Tennessee. He had twelve or so sets of lyrics I had sent his way that he had not finished.

I told him, "I'm comin' to town, and you're going to block off two full days, and I'm going to get me a hotel room not far from where you live, and we're going to work all day and into the evening, both days, till we get these done."

And he said, "Okay!"

That day, we finished "Nobody's Too Bad or Too Good," the song Karlye Hopper sang on the Hoppers' *Something's Happening* album.

"Biblically Correct" was the last one of the day. We were both tired; we had the lyric sitting up there.

For some reason, he just looked at me and said, "What kind of tune would you put on here if you were going to do it?"

Well, it looked like a quartet song to me, so I kicked off a melody and a groove. We finished it up in about ten minutes flat!

We thought it sounded like the Kingdom Heirs, and sure enough, they recorded it on their *When You Look at Me* project.

Boundless Love
Cathedral Quartet, Legacy Five, Ernie Haase & Signature Sound, Mark Trammell Quartet, Danny Funderburk & Mercy's Way, Five Broke Single Boys, Heaven Bound
See Chapters 7, 8, and 11.

Burn the Boat
The Whisnants

My brother has lots of preacher friends—pastors and evangelists—who are deeply doctrinal, old-school evangelical King James Bible preachers like he is. One of those friends pastors a little church in Mississippi, not far from Corinth. Not all that long ago, he mentioned that he was going to a hear a guest preacher at a revival meeting there.

He said, "I've never heard the preacher that they're having, but I've heard great things about him, and I'd love to hear him. His name is Brother Handley Milby. My pastor friend over there wants me to do the music. Is there any way you could play for me?"

As it turned out, I was working in Jackson, Tennessee at that time. So I parked my car at a place along the way and met Jim there. We got in his truck and drove on down to the church. I'd never been to the church before or met his pastor friend.

As we were sitting there, I noticed the evangelist over to the right. I didn't get the full impact until he stood up. He wasn't a really tall man, but he had such a presence and a dignity about him. He was a very handsome older man; he had silver hair and wore a gorgeous dark suit, a white starched shirt, and a perfect tie, just exactly like old-school preachers do. I thought, "We're going to get a good one tonight!" I just knew it.

When he got up there and stood behind the pulpit, he took his Bible and said, "Would you stand with me while we read from the Holy Writ?" I got a chill just from the way he said it.

He read from John 21, where the disciples were so discouraged after the resurrection. I honestly think those poor guys had forgotten a lot of what Jesus said was going to happen. It was like, "Okay, He's risen, but where's the kingdom? What's going on?"

He read what Peter said this way: "Well, I'm just goin' fishin'." So they went to the boat. Brother Milby made this point: The boat they found there had been kept seaworthy. There weren't any old holes in this boat; it was ready! I already knew where he was going. They had kept that boat in good repair in case they needed a plan B—in case this ministry thing didn't work out!

He really got into his point about staying with the call, no matter what. At one point he raised his right arm, made a fist, and said, "Burn the boat! Burn the plow!"

I just can't describe the feeling I had. It was more than "Oh, I can't wait to get my pen." I just *couldn't wait* to flesh that out.

He made the most beautiful case; thick or thin, good or bad, no matter what, I'm not turning back to what I used to do unless You tell me.

They finally heard the familiar voice on the seashore. It was morning time. And here's what they heard: "Children, do you have any meat?"

Brother Milby said, "What He could have said was, 'Hey, you low-down, unbelievin' faithless bunch of—I know you haven't caught anything, 'cause I know that you're doubtin'!'" I can't make it as plain as he did, but he painted a gorgeous picture of what Christ could have said. So they went over to Him and found out He had cooked breakfast—bread and fish upon the fire.

He brought more out of the text than I would ever have found! I can't think of a time when a preacher I had never heard of so impressed me with his delivery and his preaching style. As my brother would say, "He shucked the corn that night!" He got all the meat possible out of that passage of Scripture! And it was just a beautifully done message.

I knew that I had to write a farmer verse, with the plow part in there. In the bridge, I wanted to show that both the disciples and the farmer had their faith restored and stood for the Lord again.

My original title was "I Surrender All." When you hear the song, that's the last line you hear. At the time, I hadn't thought about "Burn the Boat" as a title. I thought that the whole point is about surrender.

Rick Shelton pitched it to the Whisnants. Susan Whisnant is a preacher's daughter and identified with it very strongly. I hadn't thought about preachers at the time I wrote it, and I hadn't even planned this when I made my farmer become a pastor. But how many pastors are at the point of being so discouraged that they're thinking about just quitting and going back to selling shoes or whatever? How many of them are thinking, "I just can't take it anymore! I can't take the Devil anymore! I can't take the mean deacons anymore!"

When the Whisnants cut it, Susan called Rick. She said, "I know a lot of folks are going to buy the CD on the strength of this song." But she said, "They're not going to remember the other title; they're going to want the 'burn the boat' song. So would it be okay if we changed it?"

Can you believe, the day she called, I was in Rick's office! Of course, we said yes! So it came out as "Burn the Boat" and got some nice reviews. I was thrilled that they did it; I knew Susan would have a heart for it, and she sings like an angel anyway!

Brother Milby's son, Robin Milby, has a family group with his wife and girls. When I got the demo, I got online and found how to contact Robin. I said, "I want your dad to have a copy of this, not because I wrote it, or for any other reason than this: I want him to know when he's preaching, it's not just always a lost person or a hurting church member that his message is going to speak to." I think that sometimes preachers don't realize how many ways the Lord is using them.

By Then
The Lesters
See Chapter 11.

Called In, Called Up, Called Out
Mark Trammell Trio

Kyla Rowland sent me some words on "Called In, Called Up, Called Out." She loves to write songs about hiding in the cleft, and she wrote the earlier verses. As I recall, I put a third verse in there, because if your title is "Called In, Called Up, Called Out," you have to elaborate on all three!

We wrote it totally long-distance; we were never face to face. When we got through with it, we really loved it, and we loved the demo.

That was one of the years when I took my iPod to the National Quartet Convention. Of course, I played the song for Mark Trammell. His green eyes started twinkling the way that they do when I know he's going to cut a song. When he got through, he said, "I *will* cut that song."

I said, "That sounds like a hold to me, hon!"

He said, "I *will* cut that song." He added, as he often did, "I'll be stealing a mighty good quartet song away from somebody!" (That's when they were a trio!)

Kyla and I have had quite a few cuts, but that, I think, is my all-time favorite of ours.

Can You Burn
HisSong

I was talking to Jacob Kitson at Greater Vision's booth one year at Quartet Convention. He told me about hearing a preacher preach on "can you burn," but he didn't have time to elaborate as to what direction the sermon took.

I couldn't get that phrase out of my mind. I started speculating: "I wonder what the preacher's thought was?" Well, I decided to forget about speculating and develop a challenge to Christians. Can you take the heat, 'cause it's coming? It came together quickly, and it was another one of those real, pardon the pun, smoking kind of fast songs.

It was one of the best demos I ever got from Tim Parton and Terry Franklin. One day, Wayne Haun was at Daywind. He is friends with Rick Shelton, and they work together all the time on song selection. As he was going through songs, he loved that one so much, he put it on hold himself for HisSong!

When he played it for them, they loved it and did it. I was really pleased with the cut; Wayne knows how to keep the heat in a song, and he did. I never got to hear them do it in person, but their recorded version is just tops.

City of Light
Kingdom Heirs, Melody Masters

When this one started coming, I could tell right off that it was really in old quartet style, a particular kind of old-school Statesmen song.

When Steve French called me to say that the Kingdom Heirs were cutting "I've Passed Over," he said to send him anything else I had. I sent him quite a few songs, and this was one of them. Even though I wasn't nearly as tuned into what they wanted as I am now, I already knew enough to know that this was the kind of song Arthur Rice would put over. But when I heard him sing it, that told me for sure what he could do with a song. I still love that cut!

They cut five of my songs on that record, and used this song for the title of the project. The cover, with the skyline, is my all-time favorite CD cover. They had an oversized picture of it; I liked it so much that I framed it!

Common Little Things
Kingdom Heirs, N'Harmony, Rick Webb Trio

One Wednesday night, my brother couldn't be at church. We had a precious, silver-haired, retired pastor from the First Baptist Church in Dyersburg fill the pulpit. His little wife had been in a nursing home with Alzheimer's for a long, long time. He went up three times a day, fed her meals, and lovingly talked to her. The whole town talked about how precious he was with his darling.

I had never heard him preach before. I don't remember his text, but he made his point using examples of God doing mighty things with something just ordinary. I was so impressed. We all know it doesn't take huge things for God to do something, but the way he put it was great.

I think it came together well; it said what I wanted to say. Some of the examples I used in the song were taken straight from the sermon.

When I got the demo back, I made him a copy of it, sent it to his house, and told him the story. (He knew who I was.) He was really happy about it. He has since passed away, but he went to his reward knowing he gave ol' Di a mighty good one!

I don't remember whether the Kingdom Heirs or N'Harmony did it first. The Rick Webb Trio also recorded it and sent it to radio; their version was sophisticated and jazzy. It worked, quartet or not, so I got three good cuts on that song.

Count on You
Kingdom Heirs
See Chapter 16.

Crown Him King
The Inspirations, New Gospel Singing Caravan

It's one of those that just started coming to me out of nowhere. I loved the demo. I was really surprised when I got two cuts on one Inspirations record after not having any before. It's really right for the Caravan because it sounds old. If you can write a new song that sounds old, that would be just what they need!

Deep Water
Brian Free & Assurance

Brian Free always loved this song. I haven't had a lot of cuts with him, but he did this one every time he stepped on stage for a long time. That was when Garry Jones was producing their albums. I didn't have a demo when I sent it to him; all he had was a work tape. I just loved the way Brian did it.

Do You Know What It Means?
Kingdom Heirs, N'Harmony

One day, I was just thinking about whether we even give any thought to what is involved in being a child of the King. Do we even really know? Do we really *know*? I was pondering that thought, and the song just developed from there.

N'Harmony and the Kingdom Heirs both cut it. N'Harmony's version had a great jazzy track. The Kingdom Heirs' track was straight-ahead quartet.

Even Thomas Couldn't Doubt It
Mark Trammell Trio

One day Rick Shelton told me, "Di, we've got a guy who works here in Daywind, back in the recording area. He's got a friend, and they've written a chorus to a song. They've got a great hook, and a great little chorus here, and they can't get any farther. It's called 'Even Thomas Couldn't Doubt It.'"

He played it, and it was the exact chorus you hear today. I thought, "My, my, I could do something with that!" So I put verses on it.

The Mark Trammell Trio cut it, and we got a radio single out of it!

Every Time I Call Your Name
Mark Trammell Trio

I just knew Mark would do this one. I really loved that little song. There's no real story, except when it started coming, it sounded like an old song, too. They sang that one a lot. I loved it then, and I still do.

Fighting On
The Pfeifers

One night at Quartet Convention, Mark Trammell and I were walking down through the exhibit area, looking for someone who had a CD player. I wanted to play something for him. As we were walking along together. I noticed this tall, beautiful, blonde lady heading our way.

He said, "Do you know who that is?"

I said, "No."

He said, "That's Kyla Faye Rowland."

I said, "I've never met Kyla." I had known who she was by name, and she had known who I was by name, but our paths had not crossed.

Well, he stopped there and introduced us that night. We greeted each other. Then, when Mark and I walked away, he said, "Two great ships passing in the night!" It was so funny! Those were his words, not mine.

I told Kyla, after I got better acquainted with her. She said, "Well, ships passing in the night!"

I said, "Ah, that's a good thing! That's a good thing!"

But anyway, at that time, Kyla and her husband, Bob, would take a trip over to Nashville a couple of times a year. They would stay several days and set up writing sessions for her with different people. About two months after Quartet Convention, she asked them to contact me to see if I could work that out.

I took a day off of work so that we could have the morning and the afternoon together. Of course, you get acquainted first, and we found out we have so much in common. First of all, we both brought our King James Bibles. We're both Baptists. We've both got preacher-singer brothers, just lots of things in common. We prayed before we ever started.

We talked about whether we had anything to work on. I had a part of a song that I had gotten on the way over. Back then, I rarely had pieces; it was either done, or I didn't have anything. And she had just a little bit done on her idea of "Fighting On." We decided to work on "Fighting On" first.

I did quite a bit of the words, and she did most of the tune. So it definitely has the groove and the feel of a mid-tempo Kyla song.

We've written several songs since then, but that's the first we wrote together.

I was still with Centergy; Niles Borop and the Pfeifers were close friends. The next time they were looking for songs, they just fell in love with "Fighting On." They not only recorded it, they singled it!

Kyla and I thought, "Well, we're bound to be onto something with the first one we wrote cut and going to radio!" So the song connected the two of us. We have an unusual relationship, kind of like sisters, two gals with so much in common living on opposite ends of the state of Tennessee.

I think we have only been in a room together writing one other time. Anything else we've ever done has been long-distance.

Fire Away
Kingdom Heirs

When a preacher's preaching, he never knows and cannot control what happens when the message gets out there to the congregation. He's just sowing the seed. Pastors have to learn that in their maturing process because they feel bad if they don't get a lot of moves at invitation time. The Lord has to teach 'em; you can't do that, only the Holy Spirit can.

In talking about how preachers feel and how they talk to each other, my brother will say, "We just keep shooting that ol' Gospel gun long enough, we'll hit a target every now and then!"

I thought, "Shootin' that ol' Gospel gun! I like it!" I liked that expression, and I thought about firing away.

There's an underlying encouragement for preachers to keep dishing it out straight and strong. Don't give in to the itching ears crowd; just put it right out there. They must need that encouragement because the Lord keeps giving that kind of song!

At the very end of the Kingdom Heirs' recorded version, I heard a little muffled explosion, like a gunshot. Arthur said, "Yes, the drummer on that session, in among all the accessories he has that make all the sounds that he looks for, had a sound of a musket shot." How cool is that?

Footprints on the Water
Gold City
See Chapter 18.

God Did It All
Booth Brothers
See Chapter 18.

God Has Provided a Lamb
Greater Vision

I had been to a singing. I don't know if I had heard anything that made me think about the Abraham and Isaac story. But "God Has Provided a Lamb" came together in such a way that it was just easy to get down. It was pretty much done by the time I was home!

I liked the idea that He provided the little ram in the thicket. And, of course, He provided for Abraham and He provided for us. As it turns out, I wasn't through with the Abraham and Isaac story because I have done it again since then!

It crafted up well, and I just thought, "This is right for Greater Vision. I just know it's right for them." Mark Trammell was still with them when I pitched this song; he's who I sent the songs to back then. He told me since then that he was tempted to slip it in his pocket and take it with him!

Gerald Wolfe did a great job on it. I loved the way they did it, and I loved what it said. It stayed one of my favorite ballads for a long time, and I had lots of people talk to me about it later on.

It was a neat thing to follow Gerald and Mark right off their Cathedral run and be right there on the ground floor when they stepped into Greater Vision. Of course, they came to me for songs, like the Cathedrals boys did, and I had quite a few cuts at that time.

I literally almost had to take to my bed when Mark left because I thought there wasn't anybody on the road that had the blend and the harmony that the original Greater Vision boys had. I just thought their blend was amazing, and I still think that.

God Knows How Much Mercy I Need
Mark Trammell Quartet

I wrote it on the way to a Greater Vision concert in Jackson, Tennessee. I don't remember what was in my mind, except that so often, the trip to or from a singing just triggers something in my brain, and songs just come.

I've learned that even though this song is just a simple ballad, it's still going to speak to people, and I like what it says. Even as a Christian, we still have to have mercy and grace. God knows how much to send, and at the right moment.

For years, Greater Vision baritone Rodney Griffin and I have loved to find a few minutes when we see each other to sing our new ones to the other one's face, and get feedback. What do you think about this? Do you think I have something here? Who do you think it should be pitched to? That type of thing. I sang it for him then, and he really loved it.

I wound up knowing it was going to be for Mark Trammell. When I got the demo back, it really strengthened what I thought about it. When I heard Terry Franklin start off, I knew right then, "That's Mark Trammell, dead-on, that's him!" It had the feel of some of those sweet older ballads that Mark likes to bring back.

So I sent it to him. He said, "That one's got my name on it, right there."

God Made It
Kingdom Heirs

This came out of my period of wanting to slap the face of evolution. There were other ones—"Nobody Knows the Answer but God" and "If You Ask Me"—I was just wanting to tell people, if you find something in the ground, and you don't know how old it is, and you don't know all the particulars, God made the ground, and He made the thing. Whatever it is, He made it!

The night I got the idea for that song, I was in Nashville at a singing. Eddie Crook had something to do with sponsoring the singing. This was at the venue where they used to hold the Quartet Convention, long after it had moved to Louisville. It had to be in the early 2000s because the Kingdom Heirs had already cut "I've Passed Over."

I was in the venue, and the first thing I was thinking was, "It seems smaller in here than it used to feel." Of course, that's because I had been used to Freedom Hall. During the singing, between songs, someone was talking on stage, and the song started coming to me. I reached over and jotted some stuff down while I was sitting there. When I got it finished, it had a real groove on it.

When Steve said they were going to do it, I didn't know who they'd wind up featuring. But it turned out that David Sutton was going to get the feature. I don't think it was the first single off that record, but it did go to radio.

Steve liked it because there weren't that many people just coming right out there and being really bold about Creation. That told me, early on, something that I was going to love about the Kingdom Heirs!

One of the disc jockeys from my local station, 93.1 FM in Jackson, said, "Dianne, we can't explain it, but there's a little old lady that lives in a town in our listening area. She calls every day and asks for that song. We don't play it every single day, but she never misses. It's her favorite song of all."

He said, "It's a little old lady." That struck me as odd, and I loved it, because most people who are old would not have liked a rock-n-roll-sounding Gospel song like that. They'd have liked "'Neath the Old Olive Trees" or something.

I remember thinking, "I need to know this little lady because that's the kind of little lady I'm going to be when I get old, I'm gonna be just like that! I need to go buy her a cup of coffee or something!"

God's Grace Reaches Farther
Greater Vision with Gene McDonald
Also see the story for "Heaven's Watching Over Me"

This song was inspired by the thought that, no matter how far sin can go, grace reaches farther. It's a simple melody, and it didn't take long to write.

I don't know that I can ever say all I want to say about grace. But like most Gospel songwriters, I keep trying. We'll never plumb the depths of it.

I sent Greater Vision my work tape before I ever had a demo. Gerald Wolfe had been listening to my work tapes since the Cathedral days, so it wasn't a big deal for him. And he took it! When the demo was ready, I sent that, too.

At the time, I didn't know that they were planning the *Quartets* album. (Greater Vision is a trio, and this album featured a different bass singer on every track.) I never envisioned it with a bass lead, but then, I typically write for the lead singer, and this is another one of those.

One year, when I was at Quartet Convention, Roger Talley was looking for songs for Lauren. He heard "Heaven's Watching Over Me," and we went all over Convention looking for someone who could copy the disc for him. Finally, someone told him that Wayne Haun was recording bass vocals for the *Quartets* album.

Someone said, "Dianne, this is the very night for you to go over because I think Gene McDonald is putting his bass part on 'Grace Reaches Farther.' If you and Roger get over there, I bet they'd let you in, and I bet Wayne might do a disc for you."

So Roger and I sat down, and I got to hear Gene put the bass part on that song. I'm pretty sure he did it in one take; he is Gene McDonald, after all! I couldn't see him; he was behind a curtain, but my, my, it was fun to hear him sing it.

I get a lot of requests for the sheet music to this one. Of course, there is no sheet music, but people still don't know that. They can't believe they can't find sheet music. Fans still think that if they write to the writer, I should have copies of it, and I could sell them a sheet!

The best I can send them is a lyric sheet. A lot of them, when they email me, they say, "You mean, you don't have to write it all up when you send it in?"

I say, "I don't. I play it and sing it, and there it is."

In all the movies, composers are always writing the notes right on the paper. So they have that image. I'm thinking, "You have no idea how many songwriters can't read music, and don't know one note from another, and couldn't put it on paper if they had to!"

My brother wrote two songs on one of the records my family made, and it's a wonderful song. But someone said to him, "Oh, you can't write a song! I know you don't read music!"

And I thought, "Do you think Dottie could read music? Well, she couldn't! Larry Gatlin couldn't!" They don't understand that. But people still enjoy the song.

God's Home
Triumphant Quartet

I think I had heard my brother preach one day. We hear this all the time, but it really hit home that day: "If our church building burned up, our church hasn't burned up because we're the church! We walked in here; we're the church!"

I began to think about that. God doesn't live in a building; Dagon lived in a building and fell down every time he beheld the Ark of the Covenant! That's one of my favorite stories. That old idol couldn't stay on his pedestal! How can you keep believing in one that you have to keep gluing back together because he can't stand up in the presence of God?

I can't explain *how* you know this, but this was one of those songs where you just instinctively know you can get away with a little bit of bad grammar: "God don't come in the buildin'." You would say "God doesn't come in the building," of course, but that wouldn't have been right for that song!

It came out with a driving country Gospel beat. A lot of groups liked it and held it, but didn't record it.

I played it for Jeff Stice and my Triumphant boys one day in my house. They were singing at my church that night, and I had fixed dinner. We had just finished the meal. We were in my computer room, listening; they were piled up on the day-bed, chairs, and sitting on the floor. They just loved the song; Jeff said, "We're going to do that!"

I told Jeff that I was worried it was a little too short. But they draw out the ending on their version, and it doesn't sound too short when they do it. I loved the track; they really kept it kicking when they recorded it.

God's Still Good
Gold City

I sent that to Daniel Riley. He had it for a while. The first time he listened to it, it didn't grab him. But when he listened to it again, that time it did, and he decided to record it. Aaron McCune was featured on it, and they sang it a lot on their programs.

It was on the same recording as Jonathan Wilburn's great "I'm Rich," and I loved my cut, but after I heard "I'm Rich," that's the one I kept hitting rewind on! Jonathan smoked it! But I still thought it came out good, and I thought Aaron did a great job on it.

Goin' Home Day
Legacy Five

Very few people write bluesy-type quartet songs anymore. It's my favorite kind to write because it hearkens back to when the Statesmen used to do that kind of song. To me, their "Heading Home" is the quintessential bluesy quartet song.

Arthur Rice was born to sing that kind of song. "Steppin' on the Stars" is proof of it. "Goin' Home Day" definitely had that bluesy quality. Arthur wanted to record it. Legacy Five had it on hold, and he said, "Maybe they won't do it."

I said, "Well, they will because Frank Seamans made his living in nightclubs before he was saved, and he really wants to do this song!"

Frank *did* get to record "Goin' Home Day" with Legacy Five, and he did an amazing job. I love this Legacy Five cut.

When Arthur heard the cut, he told me, "He *did* do it *that* bluesy!"

Goin' in Style

Cathedral Quartet, Booth Brothers, Melody Masters

It came along when Roger Bennett had left the Cathedrals; Gerald Wolfe was on the piano, and Mark Trammell began to screen the songs. I went to an awards show in Nashville, and took a work tape—just me playing and singing—to put in Mark's pocket.

They had already planned that Lari Goss would produce their next record. Mark liked the song and played it for Lari. Mark told me that Lari was nodding his head as he was listening, but what really hooked him in was the last chorus with the big ending. Lari thought that sounded just like the Cathedrals, and he kept it exactly like it was.

It was the title cut of that record, and they put George Younce on the feature. Of course, it never hurt for George to have the feature!

I was really pleased with the way it came out. As it turned out, that was the only time that I got to pitch to Mark for the Cathedrals because, in no time, Roger was back! So with Mark, I was one for one!

Of course, when Roger came back, he screened songs until the Cathedrals retired. I was so blessed that I could sit and play and sing, and those guys could hear the quartet potential in it. Not everyone could do that; Roger was brilliant at it, and Mark can take it from me singing it to his face, no piano. He can get it! He hears it all in his head.

Good News
Ricky Atkinson & Compassion

I had never met Ricky Atkinson and wouldn't have known him if I had seen him. But I'd been hearing their music on the radio, and I thought Ricky had one of the most gorgeous voices I had ever heard. I knew he was a writer. Some of their songs just had a different sound, not that they weren't Southern, but they were hauntingly beautiful in a different way. I was just impressed with his talent.

One year at Quartet Convention, he happened to be in his booth, and I introduced myself to him, and we got to talking. He said, "Do you co-write?"

I said, "Well, I've begun to do a little, but I don't do much."

He said, "Well, I sure would love for you to send something my way some time, to see what we can do."

With "Good News," I sent him the lyric, and he wrote the music. I think that sometimes when people write with me, they just automatically think in a quartet mode. "Good News" definitely came out quartet. Of course, he sings so well; he did his own demo. They recorded it; he even had a bass on the record where he cut it!

That was the first one we co-wrote. We've done several since.

Gospel Music on My Radio
Dean Hopper

This song has a great story, and it's not so much about what inspired it. Tim and I were living in West Memphis at the time. West Memphis had KSUD, a real strong all-Southern Gospel radio station for a small town. Of course, I listened to it all the time. I thought a guy scrolling the dials, looking for Gospel Music on his radio, would make a great song, and there wasn't anything like that out there.

I wasn't sure what I was going to do with it. But in those days, I carried around all the lyrics to my songs in a big three-ring binder. I put it in the trunk of my car. I still have the binder because I don't have all of those older songs in my computer.

Gail and I were going to go to a singing in Nashville at the time. We were going to be out so late that we were going to get a hotel room and come home the next day. (Tim had to work, and couldn't get off, but we could.)

The Hoppers were on the program, and they were also staying in the same hotel. I saw Dean Hopper in the restaurant, and he said, "Dianne, you won't believe, I am going to do a solo record! I wonder if you've got anything for me."

And I said, "In the trunk of my car, I've got something for *everybody!*"

I went out and brought the book in. We looked around the hotel and found a piano in the cocktail lounge. The lounge wasn't open, but there wasn't a way to lock the door; it was just one of those wide entrances that hotels have.

We found somebody who worked for the hotel and asked if we could turn on the light and use the room. He said, "Well, sure, there ain't nobody in this area, ain't gonna bother nobody."

So Dean and I started going through the book; Gail was sitting over in the corner. Shameless song pitcher that I am, if the lyric interested him, I just launched in and played and sang it. He loved two songs, "On Crucifixion Day" and "Gospel Music on My Radio."

He thought "Gospel Music on My Radio" was just beyond cool. He said, "That one I'm doing, that one I'm doing." And he did.

So there we were in the hotel lounge, with all the whiskey bottles back behind us! It's terrible, but that's the only place there was a piano! And we had to get it done!

He Already Sees
Collingsworth Family

I have *never* had a song—including "We Shall See Jesus"—where I received so many testimonials of how God has used the song in people's lives. People would write to Phil Collingsworth, and he would send them on to me. Time after time, this song got them through horrible times in their lives.

In fact, Kim Collingsworth told me that the song even encouraged the Collingsworths in a valley. When they received the song, they began to thank God for His mercy to get them through.

Even before the song was over, they knew that they had to sing it because if it did what it did for them, it would do that for others.

I had sent the song to Roger Talley; the Talley Trio didn't record it, but he sent it along to the Collingsworths. I later thanked him for that; it acquainted me with them, and there are no finer people. Kim is a delight in her own special way, but Phil is just the biggest light bulb in the room! He's just the cutest; he's full of energy, never anything but a big ol' smile, and a big ol' hug. Every time I see him, he just bounces up and comes to me singing "We Shall See Jesus." He holds his arm out, like he's doing Glen! I love their children, too. They're just some of my favorite people in all the world.

That's the *end* of the story. The story begins when Joseph Smith was still with the Mark Trammell Trio. Joseph is one of the most talented young men we've had; he is a wonderful writer, sings great, plays piano great, and has minister of music capabilities. One year at Convention, he brought me the idea of how God already sees the storm from the other side. He had some of the chorus and some verse lyrics, but no tune. He said, "If I send it to you, will you work on it?"

I said, "I'd be thrilled to because I love what you have."

The Collingsworth Family recorded it and sent it to radio. It didn't chart all that high, but it always went over in an amazing way to their live audiences. They told me that people have never stopped requesting that song.

I told everyone who ever talked to me about this song that I can't take credit for that great idea—it came from Joseph Smith. He just honored me to let me finish it up. Far more than any other song I've had out there, it is number one for people getting through a hard time.

He Is Mine
Greater Vision, Hovie Lister & the Statesmen
See Chapter 13.

He Picks Up a Beggar on the Way
The Kingsmen

This one was inspired by a sermon from an old-time preacher I was watching on DVD. The preacher was preaching about the journey of the Lord Jesus to the Kingdom. He charted out how Jesus was born to be a King and all the things that happened while he was on earth. At one point, he looked around, dead to the camera, and broke thought for a minute. He said, referring to himself, "You know, I sure am glad he stops every now and then and picks up a beggar along the way!"

I thought, "I just can't wait to write that!" So I did. I liked what it said, and I loved the cut. Bryan Hutson is just wearing it out.

He Rose Again
Greater Vision

Greater Vision recorded this on the first record they made with Rodney Griffin. He was featured on it, and it went to radio.

That young man is now a mega-freak-of-nature songwriter. So there's a little bit of irony here: His first radio single with Greater Vision wasn't one of his, it was one of mine! I thought that was so neat at the time, and I still do.

He Said
Gold City
See Chapter 20.

He Was in Charge
Tribute Quartet

Sometimes Kyla Rowland sends me an idea; sometimes she sends me lyrics and wants me to write a tune. This time, she just had the idea, "He Was in Charge." So I wrote a full lyric and sent it to her.

She was so excited about the lyric that she started pitching the song before she even wrote the tune! In fact, one of Southern Gospel's biggest groups put it on hold from just the lyric. We had never heard of anybody doing that before! (They ultimately didn't record it.)

Tribute Quartet cut it. Somehow, when they were getting album credits together, somebody told them that Kyla had written the song by herself! I'm sure my name was on the next printing, so it wasn't a big deal. But they are sweet, sweet boys, and they were just *mortified!* They were so apologetic. Those things happen!

He Will Be
Triumphant Quartet, Ann Downing

One day Ann Downing called me, and sang me this chorus. It was a beautiful chorus, and, of course, it was *Ann Downing*; she could sing the phone book! When someone comes to me with a fabulous chorus, it's almost always an easy thing; the music just comes. I wrote verses, and it came together really well.

So we sent it to Jeff Stice; he really loved the song, and Triumphant recorded it. David Sutton particularly loves ballads; he's a ballad tenor. It's not all he can do, by far, but it's where he shines and what he loves best.

He Will Deliver You
Kirk Talley

Kirk contacted me, looking for songs. I thought of sending this to him because he is one of the few tenors I've ever heard who honestly has *soul*. I'm talking about the kind of soul that black folks have.

Although this isn't as upbeat as a lot of the black spirituals, I thought he'd do a great job. He just knocked it out of the park! It has some high parts; I thought, "You're in your 40s, and you haven't slipped a bit on range!"

He'll See You Through
Kingdom Heirs
See Chapter 16.

Heaven on Earth
Melody Masters

The whole idea is what Jesus said in His model prayer: Let it be down here like it is in Heaven. That was God's plan in the Garden, and He's still going to get it one day! All the time, we say, "Oh, it would just be heaven on earth if I could have so and so." That's what drew me.

I loved the Melody Masters, who cut the song. Their lead singer, Scott Whitener, was one of our genre's greatest.

Heaven, the Place of My Dreams
Melody Boys Quartet, Proclaimers Quartet

It didn't have any spectacular doctrinal thought; sometimes when I get one like that, it's based more on the chords and the progressions—that old-time Statesmen kind of bluesy thing that I love to write. "Heaven, the Place of My Dreams" just fit the meter. This style song lends itself well to lyrics about Heaven.

I grieved when the Melody Boys announced their retirement because Gerald Williams would pick that kind up in a heartbeat. I don't remember whether the Melody Boys or the Proclaimers did it first. Both cuts are good.

Heaven's Watching Over Me
Lauren Talley
Also see the story for "God's Grace Reaches Farther."

I got the idea for "Heaven's Watching Over Me" when I wasn't even thinking about writing. It was really funky. When I heard Terry Franklin's demo of it, I thought, "I could hear a solo person doing this."

When I played it for Roger Talley at Quartet Convention, he thought it had Lauren all over it. This was when she was in a Dottie Peoples mode, doing more of this kind of song than she does now. Roger especially thought the line "24/7, Heaven's watching over me" sounded kind of hip, like young people would sing.

We walked all around Convention to find someone who would let us use a CD player. I only had the disc; this was before the iPod days.

After he heard it, he said, "We're going to have to find some way to record this. Somebody in this big old place is bound to have a place where I can make a disc of this and take it with me."

Well, if you're standing outside looking at Freedom Hall, the showcases are over to the right. To the left, there are some rooms that we rarely ever go in. In a room there, Wayne Haun had set up studio equipment, and they were doing some actual recording of bass vocals for Greater Vision's *Quartets* record.

When we got there, Gene McDonald was putting his bass part on "God's Grace Reaches Farther," so I got to hear Gene sing the bass part for that song.

It was such a neat moment. Roger and I were sitting there with all the other guys around. It was just one of those unexpected things that happens at Convention.

I knew he liked it when we went on a quest all around Convention to find someone who would make us a copy! He didn't even want to leave without it. So I thought, "Okay, I have high hopes for this! Roger Talley wants to leave here with it in his briefcase!" I was really tickled about that!

Sure enough, Lauren did record that song on one of her solo records. It's the only cut I've ever had on her solo records. When I heard her cut on it, even though Lauren wasn't sounding exactly like her, I began to think, "My, Wynonna Judd could wear this out!"

This is one of the best stories of all, and it has a happy ending because Lauren cut it!

Help Me, Lord
Kingdom Heirs

I didn't write this for a bass lead; I thought Arthur Rice would sing it. But when you're picking songs for an album, you can't feature the lead singer on every single song! So they looked for something for the bass man! The first time I heard Jeff sing this one, I thought, "That was a great move on Arthur's part, because he just wears it out!"

It's one of those old-time Statesmen-sounding songs. I love to write that kind!

Hey Jonah
Triumphant Quartet

I think this was the first song that Scotty Inman and I wrote together. He called me with the "Hey, Jonah" idea, and he wanted to feature a bass singer. He explained the idea, and it sounded neat: He wanted the other three singers to sustain some notes and have the bass do most of the melody.

Now this was back when I hadn't done much co-writing, and I didn't realize that Scotty was also new at this thing! When he called me, I was in the car, leaving Dyersburg, headed toward Jackson. I got excited about his idea; it just started coming, and I had a whole bunch of it written before I ever got to Jackson.

He told me that he could demo the song. At the time, their bus driver played guitar, so Scotty got him to back him up. Scotty sang all four parts, including bass. He was absolutely selling the bass lines. I have told him that if I get to live to see his children get to be teenagers, I'm going to make sure they hear it.

He said, "You wouldn't!"

I said, "It's the cutest thing I ever heard!" Still, to this day, when I play it, I get tickled! He did the three higher parts absolutely great, and he was giving that bass everything!

The guitar player was doing a certain style from the later '60s called the Memphis Sound. Artists like Aretha Franklin, Eddie Floyd, and Sam and Dave, and the Stax Records company, particularly had a special thing with horns. The Memphis Brass had a bright, trumpet-driven sound. Jeff Stice is a walking encyclopedia of all kinds of music. So I told Scotty, "You tell Jeff, and he'll know exactly what I mean, to get the Memphis Horns sound on the record." That's exactly what's on there—talk about a gal who got exactly what she wanted!

Scotty wanted Eric Bennett to love the song so much that he would say, "I just can't stand it if I don't get to sing this song!" And Eric did just fall out over that song!

When their record label at the time heard it, some of them were asking, "You really think this will fly?" It is a bit of a novelty song. Well it just went on to be nominated for Song of the Year, and it's still playing on radio!

High and Lifted Up
Cathedral Quartet
See Chapter 13.

Home Free
Triumphant Quartet, Down East Boys, John Hagee Family

It was inspired by a story of a woman who had fought major illnesses and shared with me that, "It'll be okay either way; I'll be home free." I had never heard about the other song by the same name, written by Wayne Watson, and I don't know which came first.

I wrote it in my Centergy days. The first people who cut it were the Hagee Family. Roger Talley had produced it, and it's flawless. The track is gorgeous. Matt Hagee had the lead, and they just did a stunning vocal performance all the way through. On the end, Matt went up in treetops. He's got a range!

Triumphant and the Down East Boys also cut it; it was back in the day when more than one person would cut it. It never went to radio, but it was good for me.

Homeland
Cathedral Quartet, Greater Vision, Legacy Five, Booth Brothers, Old Paths
See Chapter 11.

I Am Free
Mark Trammell Trio

The Philip Bliss hymn "Once For All" starts with the line, "Free from the law, oh happy condition." I thought that "oh happy condition" sounds so majestic and hymnlike. I wanted to enlarge on the thought and pay homage to that dear writer. He's one of my very favorites. Of course, when you start a song with a line like that, you have to *bring it* with the rest of the song!

Two or three times in my writing career, I've had Mark Trammell's face in my mind the whole time and got what I wanted. One was "He is Mine," another was "Master Builder." This was certainly another where I had his face in mind while writing. It's the old, hymnlike, deep doctrinal type of song that Mark, a Baptist preacher, would want. I thought, "I don't know if anybody will do this if Mark doesn't because this doesn't have the sound of a normal Dianne song."

I loved what Mark did with it. Back then, the Mark Trammell Trio was new; they were just beginning to get heard. I think it's one of the best cuts they've ever had. Of course, Mark was born with the voice to sing that kind (or any other!)

I Am Strong
James Blackwood Quartet

This song means a lot to me because of who sang it. James Blackwood was in the twilight of his career with the last quartet he ever had. Larry Ford was singing tenor, Ken Turner was singing bass, Brad White was on piano, and Ray Shelton was on baritone.

I was with Centergy; Niles Borop must have sent the song to them. I did not have a relationship with James Blackwood at the time. But through the process of picking and choosing songs, he called me at home a couple of times to talk about the song. He was a precious, gracious man, just like you'd expect. All I could think was, "I am on the phone with *James Blackwood!*" As a little girl who sat at Ellis Auditorium, looking straight up and hearing that precious man sing "Have You Talked to the Man Upstairs" and "I'll Meet You in the Morning"—hero doesn't even begin to describe it.

One time, I drove to Milan, Tennessee to hear them sing. I went up to James and introduced myself to him, and he was just as precious as he could be. As it turned out, he never made another record.

Did "I Am Strong" do anything? No. But it meant so much to me to have a song that he sang. Even in his later years, when his voice wasn't what it had been, it was the most touching thing to hear him sing it; it was his time to sing it.

I Believe, I Believe, I Believe
Mark Trammell Quartet

One year, at National Quartet Convention, Arthur Rice really wanted, "I Believe, I Believe, I Believe." But Rodney Griffin had heard it first and put it on hold.

When Arthur heard it on my iPod, he tried to talk Rodney into letting him have the song. Rodney said, "No, I found it first!" They were both smiling through this entire negotiation.

When Greater Vision passed on it, I still don't remember why I forgot to tell Rick Shelton at Daywind Music Publishing to hold it for Arthur.

The Kingdom Heirs weren't going to cut an album for a long time. Mark Trammell got his hand on it and cut it on *Testimony* in 2010. They did a superb job on it.

I Call on Jesus
The Kingsmen, Ricky Atkinson & Compassion

It was pitched to the Kingsmen during the Centergy days. It was my second cut with them—"Whisper a Prayer" was first—and helped open the door to the Kingsmen for me.

Ricky Atkinson and Compassion just wore it out, too. A regional group went to Ricky to produce their record and brought the song. Ricky liked it so much he put it on his own next record! That helped to introduce me to Ricky, and now we've written several songs together.

I Can Take You to the Place
Triumphant Quartet

This was another idea from Scotty Inman, and he thought the bass man should shine! We had to be careful to keep from reminding people of the old quartet song "I Can Tell You Now the Time."

If I remember right, they cut it on a record that mainly featured some of their earlier hits. But they did record the song, and Eric Bennett did get the bass feature.

When Scotty calls, I can tell when he's just bursting with an idea. He'll say "What are you doing?"

I can't think of a time I've ever said anything but, "Well, honey, I'm not doing a thing. What are you doing?" It's not like I could say, "I'm about to go into a meeting." The idea is just bursting to come out of him!

I Found Mercy
The Kingsmen

Jerry Kelso is one of the greatest melody writers our genre has ever had. He writes quartet style and not too many people do. We wrote "I Found Mercy," cut by the Kingsmen in 2006 on *Good Good God*. It's one of those songs where Jerry just sat down and started playing a gorgeous melody, and the words just started falling off of my fountain pen.

I Know My Way
The Freemans

This song was Terry Franklin's idea. He sent me an email one day: "I got kids in college, Di, I'm gonna have to start some writing! I want to send you a lyric!"

I thought, "Well, I guess I owe Terry, you know!" What a joke, like I wouldn't take anything Terry Franklin did!

If I remember correctly, he identified with this because of his dad. The original title was "I Can Make it From Here." It's about a dying man in his hospital bed.

It is the only one Terry and I have ever written together. When I found out the Freemans had cut it, I emailed him, "Now Terry, we're one for one here. In your spare time, I want you to get off another lyric to me!"

This man has no spare time! He travels the world with his wife as Heart for the World Ministries. He does demos, and he does background vocals on Daywind soundtracks. I don't think the man ever goes to bed and gets a good night's sleep!

People identify with a story of someone in their family who's about to go home. At the time the Freemans received it, Darrell Freeman had just lost his dad. They sent it to radio, and it became a top 10 radio hit for them.

I Want to Glorify My Lord / I Will Stand for Jesus
Kirk Talley, Lanna Keck

Lanna Keck was Miss Tennessee in 1997. For her talent presentation, she sang a Gospel song. She's from East Tennessee and went to Arthur Rice to produce a record for her. Arthur wanted to know what I had for a girl singer, and I thought, "Well, probably not much."

But he said, "No, she really likes the real thing. It may even be a quartet song!"

She wound up recording five of my songs. She did this one in a big-ballad style, and Arthur sang all the background vocals. Another song she recorded was "Saved"; her rendition was kind of lilting and had a whole different feel than Gold City's rendition.

Kirk Talley also cut it and changed the title to "I Will Stand for Jesus."

I Want You to Know
Kingdom Heirs

Chris Binion and I were actually in the studio together writing this one at Daywind. It was his original idea; he had the title.

When we first started working on it, I was a little bit concerned about the idea that I could tell God something; He already knows everything. We talked about that, and I said, "Well, we can almost over-analyze one to death. We're not saying, 'Lord, wait till I tell You this because You didn't know. It's almost like vertical praise; these are some things I want to say to You, Lord.'" So I became okay with it.

He had the idea for the groove; he didn't write all the tune, but he set it up. It truly was an equal collaboration, music and lyrics. When we finished it and got ready to do the work tape, one of us sang lead while the other sang backup, so Terry Franklin could hear how it was supposed to go.

Of course, when it came out on *True to the Call*, the Kingdom Heirs had that false ending, and just tore it up; it was a barn-burner. It went to radio; all the songs that went to radio from that album were top five songs.

I'm a Brand New Man
Kingdom Heirs
Also see Chapter 18.

Instead of a song about Zacchaeus being a "wee little man," I wanted to write a song about what a low-down man he was before he met the Lord. I wrote the lyric; the rockin' groove and melody are Joseph Habedank's.

We didn't have the demo at Quartet Convention that year. So I told Joseph that I was going to take him around to the Kingdom Heirs' booth and stand him up in that booth, to sing the song right to Arthur's face. I was going to stand behind him and do The Temptations-style hand-clapping and foot-tapping.

I finally found Joseph, and when I found him, he said, "I've got to man the Perrys' booth right now. There's nobody here but me, and I can't leave."

I said, "Okay, then I'm going to get Arthur."

So I walked Arthur all the way around to the Perrys' booth. Of course Joseph drew a crowd, *of course*! There he was, singing "I'm a Brand New Man." I'm in the background, doing all the finger-popping, like all those girl groups of the day. I was giving him all the help I could give him. I wish we had it on video!

About a line and a half into the song, Arthur was already smiling. I've learned to recognize his "I'm going to cut it" smile. When Joseph finished, Arthur said, "I already know what I'm going to do with it."

On New Year's Day 2011, Steve French called me to let me know that the Kingdom Heirs wanted to cut it, but it was too short. He asked if I would add another verse. So I did, and they went into the studio to cut tracks two days later!

I'm Going Home Someday
Cathedral Quartet, Gold City, Brian Free & Assurance,
Triumphant Quartet
See Chapter 9.

I'm Gonna Get Up
Karen Peck & New River

I have a childhood friend who has battled diabetes. She was going through a rough patch, health-wise, but she's such an upbeat person. She's never in the mullygrubs when you talk to her. We were on the phone, and she said, "You know, I'm just sick of feeling bad, I'm sick of dragging around. I tell you what—I'm just gonna get up!"

I knew what she meant. It was more than just rise to a standing position. It was getting up from down. I thought, "I can do something with that. I'm gonna get up!"

Karen Peck and I had been friends since she was with the Nelons. About the time I got the demo back, she was looking for songs. This was when Devin McGlamery was with her. When they heard "I'm Gonna Get Up," they just fell in love with it. Michael

Sykes produced the album, and I absolutely loved the cut. It was just cooking!

It was on the same record as "Saved." I was so thrilled to have two cuts on her record, and they were the only two that didn't feature Karen! Devin sang this one, and Susan sang "Saved!"

I found out for sure that they had done both songs when we were both at a Southern Gospel Music Guild awards show, when they were still recognizing songwriters. I was nominated for Songwriter of the Year, and Karen Peck & New River was on the program. Karen took Gerald Crabb and me out to her car. She played the rough mixes of my two and of his song, "Hold Me While I Cry."

When they came to Frank Arnold's singing in Jackson, Tennessee every year, the audience never stood up after that song. Karen said, "Dianne, everywhere we go, they go crazy for 'I'm Gonna Get Up,' they get on their feet because that's what it's about! I promise you, this is the only place we ever do this where they don't get up!"

I'm Gonna Hit the Ground Running
Kingdom Heirs

One day at work, someone used the expression "I'm gonna hit the ground running."

I thought, "Well, that would make a good Gospel song."

I thought it would be so neat to get in that gate and then just hit the ground and go right on, to see all you could see, as quick as you could. Then I thought, "Well, if it's going to be so great for this resurrected body to hit the ground running, I'll have to contrast it with how it was so hard for me to get up and going down here!"

I'm absolutely addicted to the boogie-woogie groove. My mother was a huge fan of the music of her generation, the big band music of the '40s. It is infectious. I still love the music of that period. One famous song of that era was the "Dorsey Boogie" by the Tommy Dorsey Band. It's the famous Boogie-Woogie that everyone knows; all the boogie rhythms kind of play off of it.

The boogie groove is a shuffle-type thing. Of course, the people in the '40s jitterbugged to it. It's the perfect jitterbug music. But then, along come the Statesmen and others. The Statesmen came out with an old song in the early '50s, "I Wanna Rest." The bass singer is doing that very boogie thing! It sounds so good! Anyhow, I wanted the boogie groove on this song and got it!

I had not thought about a bass lead on it. But again, Jeff Chapman was perfect to be featured on this song.

I'm Gonna Make My Getaway
Lighthouse, Down East Boys, Heaven Bound, Toney Brothers

I loved the idea of speaking of the Rapture using the imagery of getting out of prison. Except for the monster songs, this is probably the most recorded song I have ever had. Back in my Centergy days, Niles Borop pitched it to a group called Lighthouse.

They just happened to have a lead singer who *just happened* to be Doug Anderson.

I *don't* have to tell you how much soul Doug has! This version was produced by Garry Jones. When I heard their cut, I just came unglued. Their cut was so amazing that Niles started pitching. Everyone who heard it, did it, and about three groups sent it to the radio!

The first time I ever met Doug, after he joined Ernie Haase & Signature Sound, I said, "You will never know how many cuts you got for me."

He said, "I bet you're talking about 'Getaway,' aren't you?"

I said, "Yes!"

He said, "Well, I sung it that way because I loved it. I could really get into it."

I said, "Well, I would say you did!" Oh, he just wore it out!

Neither of us knew then where he would wind up, but I knew then that he had the goods!

I'm in the Shadow
Cathedral Quartet
See Chapter 11.

I'm Not Worried About Forever
Kingdom Heirs

I had quite a bit of the lyric done before finishing a tune. One day, I was coming to a session with Jerry Salley. On this particular day, I had several songs that I had quite a bit on but had not finished; that's unusual for me. I just hadn't had the time to get back to them.

I began to sing what I had on this one, and he just loved it. We finished it—not that day, but pretty soon after. We wanted it to be really quartet. Even on the work tape, I played piano, instead of Jerry's usual guitar.

That year at Quartet Convention, it happened that Steve and Arthur were both at the booth at the same time. I played it for Arthur; he liked it. I said to Steve, "I want you to listen to this one, too."

The neatest story about that song: Steve was smiling all the way through, but there came to a moment where he laughed out loud. Those dimples just opened up wide! And when he finished listening to the song, he said, "I want that song bad, and let me tell you the line that got me!"

I said, "Which one?"

He said, "I got a big house note down here, but the one in Heaven's paid for!"

I knew they would lead off with that song. And they do lead off every program with it. It's just one of those easy songs to sing, and I love the way they brought in Jeff for those bass things he did.

The little fiddle bits were a surprise to me. Jerry and I loved the way it turned out.

I'm Taking a Ride
Melody Masters

I was walking through the parking lot, getting ready to go to work, and this song just started coming. I ran into my office and got about 3/4 of it down, pretty quickly. It's an old-time quartet song. I heard an echo when I wrote it. The Melody Masters have a great cut on it, but they didn't do the echo.

Scott Whitener, one of our genre's great lead singers, was with the Melody Masters at the time. They were a great quartet. I don't know why they didn't go farther, like they should have. You never know. I also think they had one of the all-time great quartet names; it alliterated so well.

I've Got My Reservation
Mike LeFevre Quartet, Heaven Bound, Cavaliers Quartet

I wrote this song very bluesy, and that's the way Heaven Bound did it. When the LeFevre Quartet cut it, with Garry Jones producing, they completely changed the groove, making it a rockin', cookin' quartet song. I practically have two totally different songs by the same title, and I love both versions.

I've Passed Over Into Canaanland
Gold City, Kingdom Heirs
See Chapter 16.

If God Said It, I Believe It
Mark Trammell Trio

One of my honorary grandsons, Dustin Sweatman, called me with the idea. He wanted the song to be real swingy and quartety, and he had quite a bit of it done. He especially wanted the second verse to flow like it did.

At that time, he hadn't been with Mark all that long, and he was kind of intimidated to pitch the song to him. I told him, "Just do it; just walk over there and play it and sing it for him." Well, when he did, Mark loved it. They put it on their program every night because Mark liked what it said, and it suited them really well.

If You Ask Me
Legacy Five

I wrote this in the period with "God Made It" and "Nobody Knows the Answer But God" This was the third in my evolution trilogy!

I had sent Roger several songs when Legacy Five was getting ready to cut. I didn't hear anything until he called me one night from the studio. He was all excited, and said, "We've cut it, and I want you to hear it in the background, can you hear?" And of course, I loved it!

If You Give the Devil an Inch
Kingdom Heirs

Chris Binion called me with this hook. He said it needed to be the sort of jazzy quartet song the Cathedrals would sing. It didn't take long to finish. When I sent in the work tape to Tim Parton and Terry Franklin, I told them that I wanted them to think "Frank Sinatra and the Nelson Riddle orchestra, circa 1962-1963 or so." That's *exactly* what I got on the Kingdom Heirs cut ... the lush strings and brass, the subtle harmonies on the vocals. A *perfect* cut.

Innocent Blood
The Hoppers
Also see Chapter 11.

This is a deeply doctrinal song. The Hoppers will do deeply doctrinal songs because they love the Book. They'll go deep. Connie's a Bible student herself. They loved the song and recorded it, and I loved their version of it.

Back then, Connie was the only woman anywhere that was singing Dianne songs. That's changed some, but back then, she was it!

It Ain't Gonna Worry Me Long
Talley Trio
See Chapter 18.

It's Jesus
Mark Trammell Trio, Talley Trio

I wanted to write a song that went from the manger to the Second Coming. Some people say you can't do that, but it began to come together. It is possible to go all the way if you don't make it too long. Of course, with a fast song like this, you can do that.

I wanted people to keep asking, "Who is this? Who is it?" Then I wanted the chorus to give the answer. It's Jesus!

When I got through with it, I knew I had something special. Then I heard the demo, and I really knew that I did!

The first time I heard the Mark Trammell Trio's version was at Quartet Convention. I was sitting in their booth. They were tight as they could be, and the track is amazing. When I heard it, I almost came unglued. It was just flawless—the track, the vocals, the ending. They pulled out all the stops!

They sent it to radio. It didn't go that high on radio, but it did get nominated that year for Song of the Year in the Singing News Fan Awards.

Phil Cross asked them to perform it on that year's Songwriter's Showcase. He told me at that time that except for "We Shall See Jesus," it was his favorite Dianne song.

This song had a resurrection in recent days when the Talleys did it.

It's the Blood
Mark Trammell Trio

I wanted to bring out the doctrine that the works of your hands do not bring salvation. I was thinking that Adam and Eve knew all about about making an altar and offering a sacrifice. They knew it was the blood. They found out the hard way. Both little boys grew up in a home where you understood the right way to come before God. So Cain knew the right way; he just rebelled. He is the father of the whole school of thought that the works of your hands can bring salvation. I wanted to contrast the two boys and their approaches.

The Mark Trammell Trio recorded it when Joseph Smith was still with them, and he was featured. It was a beautiful cut.

The blood is like grace to me; I can never say all I want to say about it. We'll never plumb the depths.

Jesus Has Risen
Cathedral Quartet, Legacy Five
See Chapter 13.

Jesus Made a Believer out of Me
Kingdom Heirs

Someone is always saying, "Boy, that made a believer out of me!" I thought, "Well, I think that would work as a hook."

My original idea for the song was a jazzy, bluesy quartet song, like the old Stamps-Baxter tune "New Born Feeling." Arthur Rice did it like Grand Funk Railroad, with a slide guitar. It was a departure, which I loved; he loved the other kind, too, but he decided to go out of the box here. It was different from anything they had done before.

He just wears the song out; when he finishes, Steve says, "Now, don't hold back, man, just give us all you got, you know!"

Jesus Showed Up
Kingdom Heirs

One day, I got to thinking about all the times Jesus showed up in the Old and New Testaments and how things always happened when he showed up. It just came together quickly.

My brother Jim must have said something about Jesus showing up because I remember writing it on a Sunday afternoon, and Sunday afternoon songs usually come from the sermon.

This song has one of my all-time favorite endings. Hat tip to the genius of Arthur Rice!

Jesus Will
Wilburn & Wilburn
See Chapter 18.

Jesus Will Be There
John Hagee Family, Four Fold

This song was first cut by my brother's quartet. I originally wrote it in a doo-wop '50s style, and that's the way they did it. They staged it up with one man at a microphone, and the other three around the other, like the '50s. Then Four Fold came along and did it country, with fiddles. The Hagees did it straight-ahead Southern, and I loved *every* version. It was done three *completely* different ways—and all three worked!

Jesus Will Never Change
Legacy Five

Legacy Five recorded the track and the vocals for this song several years before they released it. They told me that they had decided to hold it off for another record, saving the track to put more bells and whistles on it!

I thought, "That's probably just a nice way of saying that it's not going to make it!" But then, Roger never did lead me down the primrose path!

Time passed, and I don't remember if they released another record in between. But when they recorded *Live in Music City*, the record which had "Strike Up the Band" and "The Right Side of the Dirt," Scott had promised me that it would be on there.

This is the only song I know of that was fully recorded for one project and held for another. There was life after death for it!

Jesus, I Believe What You Said About Heaven
Cathedral Quartet, The Talleys, The Trio
See Chapter 7.

Jesus, My Own
Paid in Full

I was living in Jackson, after I had become widowed, when I wrote this song. It was such a pretty ballad. I wasn't as prolific during those years in Jackson, because my work literally had me on the ropes. It was crisis mode; they needed three of me, and I just didn't have the brainpower at the end of an awful work week for songwriting! But it was written during that time.

Jeff Crews and the other members of Paid in Full have just always been precious kids in my life. They loved the song when I sent it to them, and that's the first one of mine they ever did. I was delighted with the way they did it.

Jesus, My Redeemer
Legacy Five

This one is so hymnlike, it should be in the red-back Baptist hymnal or the Broadman Hymnal! I don't remember what caused me to write it, but I remember when I got into it, the first thought I had was, "This would make a great a cappella song."

This was back in my Centergy days when I was playing piano on the demos and Terry Franklin was singing. I loved the way it came out.

I sent it to Legacy Five, and when their cut came out, it was a cappella! Scott Fowler had been with the Cathedrals when no one could get in a circle on stage and do something a cappella like "Wonderful Grace of Jesus" like they could.

I actually wrote it with the bridge the way they did it. I think they did a fabulous job on it. I always like what they do, but it's one of my favorite Legacy Five cuts.

Now that I have a beautiful a cappella cut on it, I'd love to have a big orchestrated cut. I think it would make a great choral piece. But I don't write many like that, so choral arrangers don't always think of me when they're selecting songs.

Just Beyond the Pearly Gates
Heartland Boys

This song is *so* quartet—it is one of my favorite quartet songs I've ever done. The Heartland Boys' cut is great; if it were a picture in the dictionary it would be next to "quartet, quartet, quartet!"

George Amon Webster ran the Heartland Boys. He's from Milligan Ridge, Arkansas, a small town not far from where I was raised. The town was absolutely teeming with great Gospel singers, musicians, and songwriters. My great songwriter friend Ann Ballard was also from Milligan Ridge!

George had the most marvelous stage presence and connection with an audience. The group really had a following with their live concerts. At my home church, the Heartland Boys were just about their favorites of anybody who ever came, especially when Roy Tremble was with them.

Just Preach Jesus
Kingdom Heirs

We are living in an age where many people have itching ears and don't want to hear real preaching anymore. Of course, I Corinthians tells us that God has chosen the foolishness of preaching to put to shame the wise. I have a burden about two aspects of that—the crowd that doesn't want to hear it and the preacher who still wants to deliver the goods—and, in some cases, the opposite, where preachers on TV preach all around and never even mention salvation, so people think everything's okay when it's not.

I wanted to set it up where the message could be an encouragement to preachers who might be facing congregations who are trying to subtly (or not so subtly) control what they can say from the pulpit. I wanted someone to encourage them and say, "Just preach Jesus, crucified, risen, and coming again. Preach the Gospel no matter what they say."

I had to set it up, so I could have somebody say that. So I thought, "Well, I'll have an older, mentor preacher give that advice to a younger preacher just starting out." Of course, it begs for the second verse because that's exactly what Philip preached to Ethiopian eunuch. It worked out perfectly.

The longer we go, the more courage it's going to take for preachers. From a practical perspective, here's a man trying to make a living. He has a wife, he has children, he has bills. It could get to where people say, "You're either going to preach what we tell you, or you're getting out, and we're getting someone else." I could see all that happening in my lifetime, even at my age. I hope Jesus returns before then!

I love to write songs about and for preachers. I just want to encourage them that no matter what anybody says, God will take care of you if you preach as He leads.

One thing I love so much about the Kingdom Heirs is their monumental courage about doing something that may not be popular. A lot of people wouldn't sing about a church that has called a little preacher boy aside, saying, "We don't want to hear about this." They don't shy away from that; they just courageously stand up there and sing what needs to be sung.

Keep Me on the Wheel
Gold City, Ball Brothers
See Chapter 20.

King Jesus Is Coming
Whisnants

One day, Chris Binion called and sang me the chorus of this song. I had not intended to finish the whole thing, but he had such a good chorus that it came really, really quickly. I called him and said, "Chris, you may not like this, and we don't have to keep this, and I didn't mean to finish it, but it really came, and here's what I got."

He said, "This one's done!"

I had never had a cut with the Whisnants. You know the drill—they have a woman in the group! But Chris had a very strong and long-term relationship with them. They cut it, and in the meantime, Rick Shelton sent them "Arise," and they did it, too! So I wound up with two cuts on that record.

They sent it to radio, and it went to #1. It is the only #1 song I've ever had with a woman singing it!

Know So Salvation
Legacy Five

Every year at Quartet Convention, Daywind used to take a cruise boat down the Ohio River for all the radio DJs, their artists, and their writers. The last year they did this, Rick Shelton invited me to come along and bring a friend.

Gail and I were riding along on the boat, sitting at a table with Scotty Inman. He said, "I have a chorus for you!" He started singing the chorus, and it was just killer. When he sent it to me later, it was so great, I know it didn't take me ten minutes to finish those verses!

It went to Legacy Five like a shot. They made it the title song of a custom record. Songs from custom records don't usually go to radio, but they sent this one. It got great airplay and still does!

That's the only song I ever had that started out on a boat on a river!

Lead On
Paid in Full

One day, out of the blue, Bradley Littlejohn sent me the lyric to "Lead On." I didn't know what kind of feel he wanted; I heard it edgy bluegrass. He hadn't thought about that, but when I sent it back to him, he really liked the groove. The others did, too, so they recorded it and have sent it to radio.

Let It Go and Lay It Down
Triumphant Quartet

I've only written three or four songs in my life specifically for a bass singer. This was one; I had it in mind for Eric Bennett. You can almost tell these songs because they have those echoes in them. The bass man will sing a line, and the other guys will echo.

Let Me Bring Your Children Home
Mark Trammell Trio

Mark Trammell and I love to call and talk about the deep things of the Bible. One day, we were talking about the Rapture. I don't remember exactly how he put it, but it was something like, "What if Jesus just has His foot out there, ready to step out? What if He's saying, 'Father, just let me go on ahead and go on and get Your children!'" I thought that would make a great song.

When I began working on it, I realized how much it sounded like something the Goodmans would have cut about the time they were doing "What a Beautiful Day." It just had that kind of sound.

Longing for Beulah (Land)
Gold City, Mark Trammell Trio

This was written during a dry spell when I was living in Jackson. I don't remember what prompted it, but by the time I got through with it, I knew it had Mark all over it. He was with Gold City (the lineup with Jay Parrack, Jonathan Wilburn, and Tim

Riley). You just couldn't get a bad cut out of that lineup! I still love the cut, and Mark loved the track so much that he used it again when he started his own group!

Lord, Your Word Is Still True
Kingdom Heirs
See Chapter 16.

Loving Shepherd, Gracious God
Kingsmen

David is one of the people I just long to sit with in Heaven. I want to hear him play! I want to hear him talk! I want to know what kind of mood he was in when he wrote the 23rd Psalm!

The truth of that psalm was preached out to me a little over a year ago. Brother Don Savell, a long-time friend, is an amazing preacher; people, including other preachers, come from all over the country to hear him. He preached a revival at my church, and he preached from the 23rd Psalm every night.

There's more meat in this psalm than people know; let me put it that way...and I didn't know it until this revival meeting! Brother Don said that this psalm was written from the perspective of an old sheep. And that's exactly right; it's a sheep looking back on the journey. It's not a young sheep; it's an old sheep. It's just unbelievable the way he laid all that out. I could talk about this a long time, because I am an old sheep, and He's led me through the green pastures, and He's provided for me for a long time. Now I know how David felt when he wrote those magnificent words…after the Lord had been his Shepherd for many years.

There's a tag at the end where the music fades out, and the Kingsmen sing these words a cappella: "There's a loving shepherd leading me / Where the older sheep have trod." Those words were inspired by a great man of God, preaching a very familiar Scripture passage, in a totally unique way that touched me deeply.

Mama, See the Man
The Hoppers

I wanted to write a song about the crucifixion day from the perspective of a child who has encountered Jesus before, looking on with his mama. He can't figure out why they would possibly be killing this good man. "Mama, see the man? It looks to me like He's crying."

I liked the way it moved, and I liked what it said.

At that time, I had nobody to pitch songs for me. But at some point, I got it into the hands of the Hoppers. This one's the first Dianne song they did. Connie Hopper told me that, especially around the Carolinas, where they were singing regionally, it got a lot of requests because it was just so different. It was from a different place.

This song started a recording relationship with the Hoppers. I had already made friends with Connie from way back when Tim and I went to the Inspirations' outdoor singing each summer with two or three other couples from our church.

They've recorded quite a few of my songs, starting when no other mixed groups were. Other than the Songmasters, the Hoppers were the first mixed group to ever sing a Dianne song.

Master Builder
Cathedral Quartet, Greater Vision, Mark Trammell Trio, Mark Trammell Quartet
See Chapter 11.

Mountain of Grace
The Kingsmen
See Chapter 22.

My Resting Place
Palmetto State Quartet, Southern Sound

This is old-time Statesmen! Both the Palmetto State and Southern Sound versions are just lush. This kind of song is really hard to sing because the chords are not normal, and it has to have the right orchestration. They never go to radio, but they're still my favorite to write!

Kyla Rowland likes to write "Hide me in the rock, Lord" type songs, and I like to write in-your-face "Get me on the battlefield" type songs. It wasn't like me to talk about finding a place to rest. I'm usually all about finding a place to go out there and get it preached! I don't find much of a place to sit down and rest in my songs because I'm too busy getting the preachers out there on the stump! But I love it when the Lord takes my writing style in different directions.

My Retirement Plan
Freedom

It's a great story about a poor ole boy who thought he was really going to have good benefits on the job when it all went south on him! Several of my major quartet boys passed on the song. I thought, "What is wrong with y'all? Your audiences are going to identify with this thing!"

I sent Josh Garner several songs when he started Freedom with John Rulapaugh. He just tore up "My Retirement Plan"! Early on, he was telling me that it was going to be the single. Well, Homeland liked it, but they sent out another one I wrote, "Come On In," first. Josh has told me that "My Retirement Plan" is far and away the hit of their live concerts because so many people can identify with it.

It was so timely; there were so many people who thought they had a good job and everything was going great but who had just been laid off. And I loved the upside of that, which is, "Well, I've really got the ultimate retirement plan!"

One line in the song says, "So I took out my savings, and a buddy I know said I should put it on my bills, just as far as it would go." That line is a tribute to my uncle Marvin, the funniest man who ever lived. He was my mother's baby brother, and I was the first grandchild, so there wasn't that huge a difference in our ages.

He babysat me, took me to ballgames, and taught me to drive. He was my hero; I just wasn't ready to give him up when we lost him to heart disease at sixty.

Back when people knew that a million dollars was a lot of money, they'd say, "What would you do if you had a million dollars?"

Marvin would always say, "Well, I'd put it on my bills, as far as it would go." Now you talk about a great answer—that's a great answer! I was determined to get that line in a song.

We wish we had kept a journal of everything he ever said off the cuff. None of us would ever have to work again! He was like Lewis Grizzard.

He was drafted into the Army in the '50s; they sent him to Germany. He didn't get to fly; he went across the ocean on a boat. He was seasick from the minute he got on till the minute he got off. In a letter home, he said he had six meals a day—three up and three down. They asked how he got to Germany; he said that he got there by rail. That was just the way he was!

Never Before, Never Again
Cathedral Quartet
See Chapter 13.

No Bones About It
Kingdom Heirs

Dennis Murphy called me one day, and said, "I have a great hook and chorus. My hook is 'No Bones About It.'" With a chorus that great, the verses just fell off of my pen! It didn't take me any time at all. I was just so glad that he gave me a piece of it.

No News Is Good News
Cathedral Quartet
See Chapter 13.

Nobody Ever Loved Me Like God Does
Legacy Five

Tim Parton had the idea for this song and some of the words. I fleshed out the lyric, and he wrote the melody. We wrote this when he was with Legacy Five, and they cut it. It was the only cut I got on their 2011 record *A Wonderful Life*, and I love the way they did it.

Tim and I have written two or three songs together. He's just so wonderful that anything he does is going to be good. How are you going to miss with Tim Parton?

Nobody Knows the Answer but God
Kingdom Heirs

I went through a time when I was just in a mode of being angry about evolution. I got on this thing about how they're always digging up some old bones out of the earth. They say it is a something-or-other-saurus from so many million years ago. It's always on the front page of the paper. Six months later, they'll put on the back page, it wasn't two million years old, it was a hundred thousand.

I decided to write something that basically said, if they found it in the ground, God made whatever they found, and He made the ground. And He's the only one who knows how old it was, so just get over it! That's what I was trying to say.

It was so close to the time they were heading into the studio that I didn't have a demo. So that was one of the rare times, along with "No Bones About It," when the Kingdom Heirs cut a song of mine with no Terry Franklin and Tim Parton demo, just me playing and singing.

I had sung it to Steve on the phone, and he loved it. He was in the studio, and he said, "I hope y'all like this one, 'cause we're cutting it anyway! I just wanna do this one!"

I still take the *Memphis Commercial Appeal* as a morning paper. Within a month, I found an article just like that. Deep in the paper, there was an article retracting an earlier claim, saying that a certain fossil wasn't as old as they had thought. I cut it out and sent it to Steve French. All I wrote across the top of that article was, "Nobody Knows the Answer but God!"

In my period when I was shaking my fist at evolution, "God Made It" was the first one of those songs. Steve knew I had written others about evolution. After the Kingdom Heirs cut this one, he said, "Well, Di, you think you got that out of your system?"

I said, "I don't know!"

He said, "Well, if it's not, don't worry about it. Just keep right on till you get done!"

Nobody's Too Bad or Too Good
The Hoppers

Everyone has gotten email forwards of church signs, and that's where this title came from. Nobody's too bad to stay out, nobody's too good to come in.

I thought, how can I make it into a song that's not too preachy? What can I do with the lyric? I wanted to reach people who seem to think that they can worship just as well at home without having to assemble. Of course, we have Scripture that says we are to assemble. So I thought, "I want to not be preachy about the people who don't, but I want to extol the virtues of what you get from going."

This was one of the songs Rusty Golden and I finished in our two-day marathon writing session. I came to Nashville, got a hotel room, and I told him I wasn't leaving town till we got done! I said, "I don't care if it kills you, I don't care if it kills me, we're gonna finish!" Well, it nearly did kill us because we finished up twelve songs in two days!

When he started playing this one, I didn't expect that kind of groove, but I liked it. When we got to the tag, I heard his music to "Losers and winners, saints and sinners, are welcome in," and thought, "Now that's cool, right there."

The next time Quartet Convention came around, he worked diligently to put all of our finished songs on CDs, with labels and cases with contact information, and dropped them off everywhere. He left one with the Hoppers, just like he left one with just about everybody else.

There were two other songs that caught their attention, one Connie Hopper loved and one Dean Hopper loved. When the record came out, they hadn't done either, but they did "Nobody's Too Bad or Too Good."

I was pleasantly surprised; that is the first song they've ever had that features little Karlye. She just sings it so sweetly, and when they do it on stage, she does it with her Mom and Dad. They even sent it to radio!

Nothing Was Burned
The Perrys

Kyla Rowland and I had already written a Hebrews in the fire song. I wasn't going to do another, but she is just eat up with the Hebrews in the fire! She called me after she heard a preacher preach on the thought, "nothing was burned but their bands."

I thought "You know, we might could do something with *that*!" She sent me most of the words; I think I added a third verse.

She wanted a song that would feature the bass man, really like a quartet, and as it turned out, that's the way Tracy Stuffle set it up on the stage: "Well, I always wanted to be with a male quartet, and this sounds like one they'd do." Then Libbi goes off in the corner and starts texting on her cell phone.

I thought, "Well, Tracy, if you'd wanted a song like that, you should've come to the quartet girl a long time ago! I've got a lot of 'em!" Of course, I didn't say that!

It's the first and only Perrys cut I've ever had, and I always knew if I slipped in, I'd slip in on Kyla's coattails. We laughed about that. I said, "If I ever get a Perrys cut, I'll have to slip in with you."

She said, "Well, is it time for me to say the same thing about the Kingdom Heirs?"

I said, "Well, we'll just hope for the best!"

The Perrys don't always put songs on hold; sometimes they just go into the studio and cut the songs they like. I hadn't heard anything from them for a while. One day, I got a text from Joseph Habedank, and he said, "Is 'Nothing Was Burned' yours? We just cut it this morning." So I found out through a text message that I had my first Perrys cut. It was about the nine millionth one for Kyla, so it was old hat for her!

Now He Knows What Heaven's All About
Triumphant Quartet

Scotty Inman called me with the idea. He had either been to a funeral for an elderly preacher, or he knew someone who had.

When the preacher's family was leaving the church where the funeral was held, one of them said, "After preaching about it all these years, now he knows what Heaven's all about."

When Triumphant Quartet was listening to songs for their 2005 project, Clayton wanted to sing it. There was only one problem: I had written it in the first person, like the preacher's son was telling it. Clayton's daddy wasn't a preacher, and so he asked if I could tweak the song to where it didn't sound so autobiographical. I reworked some pronouns so that he could sing it with more validity.

Of Thee I Sing
Greater Vision, Ball Brothers

When I wrote the song, I heard the whole arrangement in my head, and I knew Greater Vision was the group to do it. When I was ready to send it, I didn't just want to send in me singing; I knew I needed to play it so they would know the chords.

At this point in the early '90s, Aunt Mavis, Mama, and I were doing a little singing again and having a lot of fun doing it. So I asked them if they would learn it so we could sing it together. Well, it was hard, and the Ross Sisters never thought *anything* was too hard because we tackled Goss Brothers arrangements! We learned it over a short space of time; it wasn't one we'd sung forever, like all those we'd sung back in our heyday. It was a little work for us to get it like we wanted it, but we did. We went to Aunt Mavis's house in Blytheville, I played her piano, and we sang it and sent it to them.

When I heard their record, it was just perfection. I asked Mark how long it took them to get it right, and he said, "Well, actually, we got it on the first take."

I came back and told Mama and Mavis that, and they said, "Yeah, but they had our tape to go on, that's why!" Oh, how Mark laughed when I told him that!

They said that with all kinds of affection because they adored Greater Vision. Nobody in the world would tease those two gals like Gerald Wolfe could, but they adored him, so he could get away with it!

Oh Come Along
Cathedral Quartet
See Chapter 13.

On Crucifixion Day
Dean Hopper
See story for "Gospel Music on My Radio."

On the Gloryland Way
Kingdom Heirs

I wanted to do a little quartet song inspired by the hymn "Gloryland Way." I don't have to labor and toil over this kind of song; I can't explain why, but it comes easily.

I thought, "This is so Kingdom Heirs!" Arthur Rice picked the demo right up. I just knew they would lead off their concerts with it, and, in fact, they did, until the next album came out.

Once for All
The Hoppers

This came out of a study of Hebrews. I knew it sounded like a hymn, and it was the deeply doctrinal type the Hoppers love.

Wayne Haun told me later on that when they were listening to songs, they were listening to some really ornate demos and some really rocking demos. When they came to this one, since it was a Centergy song, it was just me on piano and Terry Franklin's vocal. When they played this one, Wayne said that it hit him between the eyes. He said, "I want y'all to do this one for me. I want to work on this." And, of course, his orchestration was just flawless!

If someone with an ear like Wayne Haun or Lari Goss sees what's in a song, you know you have something. I absolutely love the way it came out.

Peace Like a River
Greater Vision

This is one of those songs like "There Is a Haven" or "Loving Shepherd, Gracious God." When I finish them, I think, "Well, it's not dramatic enough." Sometimes the Lord has to remind me that they're not all supposed to be "We Shall See Jesus"—that a lot of people like this kind!

By the time this came out, I had signed with Daywind Music Publishing. And with all the years Greater Vision had been with Daywind Records, they had never cut a Daywind Music Publishing song. (Rodney Griffin has his own publishing.) Ed Leonard thought he was never going to get a Daywind song on one of their records! This was the first!

Peter, James and John
Gold City

One day, I was riding along in my car. I started singing, from nowhere, "One man was praying, three men were sleeping, one was betraying the sinless Son of God." When that came out of my mouth, I thought, "I'm supposed to contrast the five principal players of the night before the Crucifixion."

The next line that came was "They'd left that last supper." Well, we don't know where Thomas and Bartholomew went. But we know what Judas did, we know what Peter, James and John did, and we know what Jesus did. So those were the principal players.

It had a groove that sounded so much like the Oak Ridge Boys. It didn't sound particularly like anything I would usually do. When Steve French heard it on the radio and fell in love with it, he didn't recognize it as one of mine, and he almost always can tell!

When I got to the verses, I thought, "Okay, now I'm supposed to pull this into the context of the professing church, and where do we fall in that? Would we be the ones who stay in the garden, ready to fight and stand between Jesus and the soldiers if we had to, at our own peril, or would we be the one that went all the way to the Cross?" Obviously, even Jesus' siblings weren't there. He turned his mother over to John.

Then, of course, Judas was the villain of the piece. What an amazing contrast...the Son of God and the son of perdition. Judas was the only human person that was ever called the son of perdition, and Jesus called him a devil, so I think that says it all.

The song didn't take all that long to write. When I finished it, I knew it was something special. Adam Kohout recorded the track. He's great on piano and drums, but he gets guitarists, fiddlers, whatever he needs, and does a marvelous job of interpreting the feel of the song to the instrumentation. Then, of course, Terry rises to the level of the track vocally. However great the track is, he will be that great with his vocals.

When I got the demo, more than any song I've ever gotten a demo on, it truly could have gone to radio just as it was. It came in the day before Gold City was going in the studio. When Rick Shelton heard that demo, he got in his car, drove across town with it, and put it in Ken Harding's hand. (Ken Harding heads New Haven, Gold City's label.) Ken played it, and Rick said, "Do you think they'll do it?"

Ken said, "Oh, yes, they'll do it!" He knew it would be right for them. We had already been 99% sure we would get a cut on that record with "Footprints on the Water," and they cut this one, too.

I still remember the red-letter day when I got an email from Danny Riley, "Dianne, guess what! 'Peter, James, and John' is the first single." My first thought was that it was a lot of pressure because Gold City hadn't had a charting song in a while. It was going to be a really pivotal thing; there was a lot riding on it, and if it didn't do well, I was going to feel really bad!

It's the fastest-rising single I've ever had. It went from twenty-four, to seven, to three, to one. I'm not going to say that I wasn't glad for myself, but I was *thrilled* for them! Their last #1 hit was "He Said." That was mine, too, so I thought that was a nice little piece of continuity there.

People have told me they had to hear it a second or third time to really dig down and get into the storyline. I think when you first hear "one man was praying, three man were sleeping," you almost have to get to that last supper bit before you know who was sleeping and Who was praying!

At Quartet Convention last year, Gold City sang it at every stand they had. Two ladies there stopped me and said, "We want you to tell us about that song. We love it, but we're not sure we get it completely." You never know the level of someone's Bible knowledge. I had the thrill of getting to talk to those ladies about that and seeing the light come on in their faces.

I thought Daniel Riley did a great job on the cut. Their tag ("Jesus chose twelve men; almost all of them were faithful") wasn't on the demo, but ending it with that thought-provoking line was a great idea. It's been a big song for them, and I couldn't be happier.

Pray for Me
Ernie Haase & Signature Sound, Kingdom Heirs
See Chapter 16.

Praying Your Troubles Away
Kingdom Heirs

Jerry Kelso is one of a small handful of writers who actually came to my house in Dyersburg to write. Most of the time Dianne gets to drive all the way to Nashville and back, get a hotel room, or drive west into the setting sun! But hey, it's worth it—it's all deductible!

One day, Jerry came to my house, and we wrote two songs. He came in with the complete intricate melody to "Praying Your Troubles Away." He didn't have a single word, just the tune.

It was a Wednesday morning; I never will forget, I said, "Jerry, you don't even have a title in mind! Nothing! We're never going to get this done!"

Well, I thought of "Praying Your Troubles Away." Through that day, I managed to come up with all the lyrics but a second verse.

We actually stopped at one point and finished another song, "Jesus, You're My Hero." That one wasn't hard to finish.

It got to be time to go to church. I said, "I have to play at church, so you stay here, and see what you can come up with." So I went on out to the church and got home around 7:30. We worked on that thing till about 10:00 at night and finally got it finished. We got a fabulous demo from Tim Parton and Terry Franklin, and the Kingdom Heirs did it just like the demo.

Roll On
Legacy Five

My mother grew up in the big band era and loved that music. She had a lot of big band records. One from back then that I fell in love with was Tommy Dorsey's band playing the "Dorsey Boogie."

In the early 50s, the Statesmen and other quartets borrowed heavily from that groove. The bass singer would do with his voice what a boogie pianist would be doing with his left hand. When I was hearing "Roll On" in my head, I was hearing a heavy boogie groove.

Scott Fowler put the song on hold when I sent it to him. They did it, and they're still doing it live on stage. They've even done it on the Grand Ole Opry!

Steve Mauldin produced the record, and what he heard was a little dash of Texas swing. It worked. It's just interesting what an orchestrator or producer will hear out of something like that. I absolutely loved it, and it was a wonderful cut.

Safe On the Glory Side
Mark Trammell Trio

This is one of my testimony songs. I wrote the tag—"When you walk beside my coffin, by then you'll know I'm walkin'"—for all my friends if I pass on first. The song started coming pretty quickly, and I could tell it was strong.

When I go to see the Booth Brothers in concert, Jim Brady and I like to talk about songs. One year, when I went to see them at the Frank Arnold concert in Jackson, Jim asked if I had anything new, and I said, "Well, yeah, I do, but I kind of hear it a little bit bluegrass."

He said, "Well, sing it to me," and I did, and he just lit up. He said, "The Booth Brothers would record that. Not really grass, but we'd record that. When you get the demo, I'd sure like to have it." Jim doesn't put a song on hold until he talks to Michael and Ronnie Booth, but he really liked that song.

It's not very long from the Frank Arnold concert, which is in July, till Quartet Convention. I didn't have the demo by Quartet Convention. But Mark Trammell was looking for songs, and I was at his table singing songs to him. I really wanted his opinion on this one; I was trying to reconcile it in my mind because I heard it pretty grass. I told him that Jim was excited about it and asked what he thought the two Booth boys would think about it.

I really wasn't pitching it to Mark; I had *no idea* he'd want a bluegrass song! I started singing, and there's a twinkle that comes into his eyes when he gets excited about a song. I saw that twinkle. He started grinning, and when I got to the tag, he just was all over himself.

He looked at me dead in the face, and said, "If you sing that for anybody else this week, I'm going to break your legs."

I said, "Are you telling me you want this song?"

He said, "I'm telling you I'm going to record that song."

I said, "What are you going to do about the grass part?"

He said, "I'll put some grass on it, I don't care! I want it!"

He then said, "Did Jim Brady put it on hold?"

I said, "No."

He said, "Well, *I'm* putting it on hold!"

Rick Shelton came up later in the week. He brought some discs that included the demos. He told me to meet him at one of the side doors, over where all of the buses park. Not far from where he came in, some people had a CD player and said we could use it.

I had little earphones on so nobody could hear but me, and I was listening to "Safe on the Glory Side." Terry Franklin did the vocal, and I think Andrew Ishee did the piano track. He did some piano demos for Daywind songs while Tim Parton was with Legacy Five. It was just a killer demo, everything I wanted. They were just wearing it out.

I was just having a time over there, and I didn't realize it, but I was drawing a crowd! Enough of them knew who I was to know I was hearing one of my songs for the first time. When it got through, probably about ten or twelve people were watching, and they said, "Boy, we want to hear that one!"

I said, "Well, with no false modesty, you sure do! It came out just like we wanted it to!"

Then we hunted up Mark. It was on a disc with three or four others. It was the only copy I had; I was going to listen to them on the way home. When I got to Mark's booth, he put it in his coat pocket! He said, "You're not taking this home! *I'm* taking this home!" And I said, "Okay."

I told this story at Phil Cross's Song of a Lifetime showcase the next year. I just laid it out there, and the audience loved it. I said, "We talk to each other that way, always talk about breaking legs, and sending the Mafia over to your house, all that, if you don't cut this, or if you sing it to somebody else."

When Mark says something like that, his face is sober as a judge. He said, "Nobody else better hear that this week," and then he took the disc to make sure!

Their tenor singer, Eric Phillips, did a fantastic job. In fact, if they had been as well known then as they are now, it would have gone to #1 because that's how strong their cut was.

They were going to do it as grass as I wanted, but when they showed up for the session, the grass pickers didn't show up. So it just came out more of a driving, rock-Gospel thing. But if you notice, they bend the notes just a little. So I told the crowd at Song of a Lifetime that they did that just to please me because the grass boys didn't show up!

I asked Mark some time ago if he and the guys would sing that song at my funeral, if I have to have one. (I really hope I don't —I hope I go in the Rapture!) He said he would. I said, "I don't want you to tame it down; I want the real scaldin' track! I don't want that sad stuff! I want that!" He promised me he would come, and they would do it just like I wanted them to do it.

It is one of two strongly personal testimony songs of mine. The other is "When You Look at Me." I've approached Arthur Rice to sing that at my funeral because it truly is my testimony; he also said he would.

I've loved "Safe on the Glory Side" from the beginning, and I've loved the way it came out. It's a song about eternal security! Saved and safe!

Salvation is the Miracle to Me
Legacy Five, Kingdom Heirs

I don't remember what inspired the song, but I guess it is as much absolutely quartet from start to finish as any other one I've ever done. It's one of those right-in-the-pocket quartet songs. The Kingsmen could've done it, Triumphant could've done it. Anybody in the world that knows how to sing those backup echoes could've done this song and done it well, but the ones who did it did a great job!

Legacy Five cut the song first. I had written some echoes into it, and they did those. When the Kingdom Heirs cut it, Arthur's arrangement actually broadened the echoes and put more words in, and it really sounded old-time quartet. I loved both versions.

Saved
Gold City, Karen Peck & New River
See Chapter 20.

Since Jesus Moved In
Kingdom Heirs

I remember thinking at the time I was writing it, "This is the Kingdom Heirs. It's exactly the kind that they do, and nobody else really does these like they do."

Another thought I had was, "This will be a perfect lead-off song for them."

It was hard to write because I started out doing a couple of quick internal rhymes together in a line. The closer rhyming words are to each other, the harder it is! I almost painted myself into a corner trying to finish that one. I was pleased with the way it turned out; they did a great job on it!

Since Jesus Touched Me
Gold City

I wrote both "Since Jesus Touched Me" and "Keep Me on the Wheel" right before Quartet Convention one year. I actually wrote one of them on the way to Louisville! When I made it in, Mark was at the Gold City booth. I sang both of them to him, and he put them on hold right there, just from me singing!

He said he liked the different scenarios in the verses and thought that each one could have a lead. He said he'd like Tim to start it off, singing the story of the demoniac man. Mark sang the second verse, and Jay Parrack sang the third.

It's one of those knock-him-out quartet songs, and I thought it might have been single-worthy. At one point Tim Riley told me that they had performed it at a Gaither taping. He said, "You know, that don't mean nothin', but it sure did sound good!" The song didn't make it onto the video, though.

So Long and Goodbye
Kingdom Heirs
See Chapter 16.

Sooner or Later
Danny Funderburk

I don't get many cuts from soloists; most of my songs aren't written for soloists. Ivan Parker cut one of mine, and Karen Peck did a solo record at one point, and I have a song on there, too. Danny Funderburk put this on what I think was the only solo record he ever did.

It was a little rock-flavored thing. Of course, he was used to singing that kind of mine, since it had a "Master Builder" feel to it.

It doesn't matter when Jesus comes; He could come right now. Nothing has to happen first. He could come sooner or later without messing up God's clock at all. So I liked the hook, and I still do.

I was pleased with the cut; Danny Funderburk never did anything poorly!

Steppin' on the Stars
Kingdom Heirs

I was going to a writing session at Daywind with Niles Borop, my former publisher. I hadn't seen him in a long time.

As so often happens, I started getting it in the car. I don't know why; I wasn't thinking about the planets. I couldn't even tell you where it came from. I started singing it, and I pulled a little tablet from the glove box. (I've done it on the interstate, I'm sorry to say. I'm careful; I'll just jot a note to know what I'm doing.)

I got so much of it written that I almost laid it aside when I got there. But I hated to show up at a session without an idea!

It turned out to be very bluesy. When Niles and I finished it, we were both happy with it.

I could just tell it was one Arthur was going to fall in love with. And when he really loves one, when he's dead set on one, he'll write back and say, "Did you even have to ask if I wanted to hold it?"

I love the song's imagery. It talks about the part of God's creation that just fascinates astronomers.

This song is one of Arthur's stunning vocal performances. Just perfection!

Strike Up the Band
Legacy Five

I was on my way to see the Kingsmen at a little church about ten miles from my home. I was ridin' along in my car, and here it came: "Strike up the band."

And I thought, "Oh my! Strike up the band—that's what's going to happen when we hear the trumpet." Well, I had everything but the second verse done before I got to that church, ready to jot down on my little book.

The Kingdom Heirs did one of mine called "Lord, I Always Know That I Can Count on You." I also wrote that on the way to a Kingsmen concert. But neither song got pitched to the Kingsmen because they weren't looking at the time. So I've always thought I owed Ray Dean Reese two that he didn't get!

Sweet Gloryland
Perfect Heart

This goes back to the start of my relationship with Niles Borop, after I met him at a Phil Cross songwriting seminar. When he was telling me he'd like to work with me, he said, "Well, just send me something along, and we'll see." So Sweet Gloryland, a straight-up convention song, was the first thing I ever sent him, and he got it cut by Perfect Heart! So this song started our publishing relationship.

We were one for one. I was kind of green; I'd never had any idea that somebody could run a publishing company for Southern

Gospel music and just make their living off pitching my songs. I thought, "How great is that? Every one I send off, he's going to work it, and it's going to get cut!" So this was another place in my writing life when I was still green!

Of course, Jeff Stice and I have been friends for a long, long time. It's the first cut I ever had with a *quartet* with Jeff Darlin' Stice at the piano, so it's also memorable to me for that reason.

Sweet Heaven, My Home
John Hagee Family

This isn't even a quartet song as much as it's truly a convention-style song. It ought to be somewhere in the *Heavenly Highway Hymns*, the singing convention songbooks.

The John Hagee Family cut this on a record that had three of my songs. I was talking to Matt Hagee at the Quartet Convention a year after it came out. I had not met him before. He was just a delightful young man; I enjoyed visiting with him. I told him how honored I was to get songs on a Hagee project because I had a pretty good idea of the kind of sifting process that Brother Hagee did on the lyrics.

He said, "Oh, you have no idea!" They give Pastor John all the lyric sheets, and he just makes a pile on the floor of the ones that aren't doctrinally sound. Matt said that sometimes he doesn't have to read very far before they go on the floor!

He saves the others and puts checkmarks on the right-hand side of the top of the sheet, so everybody knows that they passed.

They don't even consider the songs till they see the checkmark. I was really tickled that I got a checkmark on three out of three!

It sounds so much like an old convention song that Brother Hagee thought it was! As they were practicing on it, he looked at the kids, just smiling while they were singing. He said, "I love this song; I've always loved this song."

They started grinning.

He said, "I love—I've never heard this song, have I?"

They said, "No, Daddy, you haven't! This one is a new song!" It thrilled me that he thought it was an old song; it made me think of the time McCray Dove looked all day long for "Oh Come Along" in the old convention songbooks!

Heaven just lends itself so well to convention songs. They just go together; I don't know why.

Sweet Land of Rest
Palmetto State Quartet, The Kingsmen

I have written medium tempo ballads that are kind of vanilla, like "There is a Haven" and "Loving Shepherd, Gracious God." This one wasn't like that. On the demo, Terry Franklin's vocal just soars up high. It gave me a chill!

This is when Phillip Hughes was singing with the Kingsmen, and Tim Surrett was picking the songs. I sent them several. Tim just loved that song, and here's what he said about it: "You know, Dianne, this is one that Foxy would have written." (Eldridge Fox, late owner of the Kingsmen, went by "Foxy.") I loved that comparison!

I've loved every Kingsmen cut I've ever had. But if you pulled a gun on me and made me pick a favorite, it would be a hard call between this one and "Mountain of Grace." This is the one of theirs that I play the most.

Later on, when Palmetto State requested I send them songs —when John Rulapaugh was with them—they asked me about that one. They loved it. I said, "Well, I have to tell you, the Kingsmen did it."

They said, "We don't care, we're going to do it anyhow." I love their cut, too.

Tell Me Who
Cross 4 Crowns, Melody Boys Quartet

The Melody Boys and Cross 4 Crowns both cut this one. Arthur Rice produces so many albums that he keeps a huge stash of my songs on hand that the Kingdom Heirs have never cut. He played this for the Cross 4 Crowns boys, and they cut it. It's just a spectacular cut. Justin Terry, the group's bass singer, he did the job!

Tell Me Why
Kingdom Heirs
See Chapter 16.

Tempted Like Me
The Apostles

This one is just kind of different, and I've always loved it. I didn't know if anyone had ever looked at all the ways Jesus was tempted. I don't think temptation always means temptation to sin, but perhaps temptation to indulge yourself a little bit, and He never crossed that line at all. He could have thought, "I don't have a family, I don't have a home to go where there's a wife and some children. That's not My life; that's not going to be for Me." But that never tempted Him to stray in any way.

I was trying to get across that depth of what it means when the Bible says that Jesus was tempted in all points like we are. That's what makes Him such a marvelous, great High Priest. He's been through everything. No wonder He can advocate for me so well when I'm discouraged or when I'm tired; even the ministry can wear you out sometimes. He had to walk everywhere He went. There was no real comfort. We don't hear about nice hotels and fabulous meals. It was very humble fare for Him. I just thought, "We know the ultimate sacrifice He made. But He sacrificed His whole adult life." I wanted to say that, and I just think it was a pretty song.

I didn't know if anyone would record it because it was a little far-out. But that's what I've spent a lifetime doing, if I felt like I could get away with it.

That Little Baby
Gold City, Kingdom Heirs, The Ruppes
See Chapter 20.

That Old White Flag
Triumphant Quartet

As Scotty Inman puts it, this song has taken on a life of its own. It's the only song I've ever written that honestly has taken on a life of its own.

My brother has a very colorful way of preaching. He inspires so many of my songs with things he would actually say. When it was altar call time, he would say, "Why don't you wave that old white flag of surrender, get down here in this altar, and do business with God?"

I thought, "If I could write a song about conviction and salvation, that would be a good expression to use. Just wave that old white flag." It's all about surrender. I can't go any further. Here's the flag, I'm waving it! I'm giving it up! I started developing that thought, and it came really quickly.

Early on, when I got the line about being so close to Hell you're about to fall in, I thought, "I'm not going to get anybody to sing THAT! Some people don't mind the guy in the song being lost, but they don't want him being THAT lost!" But my Triumphant boys don't mind singing that line because some people are just that lost!

I could tell right away that it really came out bluegrass. When they were looking for songs, it was so new that I didn't have a demo yet. I had to send them a work tape; those poor boys have heard me before, and they have to hear past that!

On all my work tapes, I give instructions, and I said, "Now Jeff, Darlin', this one is all the way bluegrass, and a Kentucky boy like you is going to have to keep it grassy if you do this song."

He called me and said, "We love the song!"

I said, "You gonna do it grassy?"

He said, "I *promise* you."

I said, "You mean to tell me that I'm gonna get a dyed-in-the-wool Southern Gospel quartet to sing a bluegrass song?"

He said, "That's exactly right."

Clayton Inman told me later they all loved it. They pick a song when one of them feels the nudge to say, "You know what, I think I'd kind of like to sing that."

Nobody had spoken up. Clayton was just waiting to see because he really wanted to do it, but he is the dignified sort that looks like he was born in a three-piece suit. So he said, "I'd like to do that," and they said "okay."

The little a cappella bit at the beginning was their idea. I didn't write that in, but it was absolutely inspired.

When Jeff sent me the song, the first time I heard it, the hair stood up on the back of my neck! The harmony was so tight.

When I heard the real grass treatment, I just couldn't stand how fabulous it was.

My phone rings with it; it's been my ringtone ever since my niece, Rachel, figured out how to get it on there. It makes me smile every time my phone rings.

Triumphant was with Daywind at the time. I think the suits at Daywind thought that I had lost my mind, and they had lost their mind! They just couldn't quite catch the vision at first.

When Triumphant started doing it live, audiences liked it, but it was kind of a shock to them. I'm not sure what actually led Clayton to start the moves, but the more he did, the more it began to take off. Now the real Clayton is not this way, but on stage, he just looks so dignified, like he ought to work at Chase Manhattan Bank!

When he started doing *Oh Brother, Where Art Thou*, which is exactly what he's doing, people went nuts. Nuts. And the more they went nuts, the more it egged him on!

Then they built this whole little act around where Jeff would pretend to pout because there's no piano in bluegrass. So he has to act like he hates it. In fact, they always set it up like they hate it. When Eric Bennett starts saying, "Well, I guess it's time that we have that song," the crowd is going nuts!

Eric, David Sutton, and Scotty stand there just as sober-faced as the Dillard boys, who played the Darlings on the Andy Griffith Show. (The Darlings never spoke a word or cracked a smile.)

They have never stopped singing it, ever; they'd be run out of town on a rail if they didn't do it! We've set Clayton up with a song he can't quit singing.

It was nominated that year for Song of the Year in 2009.

It's been as much of a huge thing between Clayton and me in its own way as "We Shall See Jesus" was between Glen and me. It's been a career-defining signature song. And it even shows the fans a Clayton they had never seen.

Clayton has told me so many times, "Dianne, people might think I'd get tired of singing that song. I have never, ever not been excited to sing it. I have as much fun every night as I did the first time I sang it. It is endlessly fun for me."

One other story: When my brother was still preaching at my church, Springhill, he also directed the choir. He wanted his choir to sing the song to that scalding track one Sunday morning. Of course, I have tons of friends in the choir. Here came these elegant ladies, professional women, with their beautiful pearl earrings and choir robes, marching out there. You expect them to sing "Majesty" or "Old Rugged Cross," and here they're going, "Why don't you just wave that old white flag of surrender!"

I told Clayton, "I kind of have a feeling that no church in the United States of America has ever used 'The Old White Flag' as a choir special right before preaching."

And Clayton said, "You know, they should, it's about getting somebody saved!"

I said, "Yeah, I know it. That groove would throw a lot of people off, but not Jim Branscum!"

This is another one I listen to over and over. I never get tired of the recording. I have had people tell me this, though: As much as they loved the fun that everybody has with it, it really does have a serious message, and they like to listen to the record to reinforce it.

I don't use the term magical because God has everything to do with it, but it's been one of the huge ones in my writing life, probably in the top three or four of the ones I'll be known for someday.

The Church Will Overcome
The Talleys

I wanted to show that no matter what the Devil does, no matter what ammo he brings out, he will fail, just like he failed in the early church.

I still remember sitting in my chair, thinking about the first verse. When the line came that said "The lions couldn't tame it, the fire couldn't quench it," I kind of got a chill. Then when the line came, "Nero had a lot to learn / there's some things that just won't burn," it was one of those moments when the hair on your neck stands up a little bit! The lions couldn't tame what these people had! There are some things that won't burn!

I had the idea of putting Bible heroes in there as an echo. When I got to Elijah, then I thought, "Well, I have some choices here," but I had to meter it out. Jeremiah worked just fine.

I wanted to do the second verse about the church now. I thought, "Well, I'm just going to get in people's face about the false religion and who the enemy is using against us now—and how we're going to overcome that, too!"

It was a fun song to write.

The Devil has never been successful in prevailing against the church. He wasn't then. He wasn't in the Dark Ages. And he's not going to be now. I wanted to say it vividly, and I wanted it to really move and shake. It was special from the outset, and the right folks got it.

The Cross Became My Saving Grace
Wilburn & Wilburn

When I wrote the lyric, I was purposely not letting any tune get in my mind. Joseph Habedank and I had finished "Footprints on the Water," and I thought, "You know, I bet Joseph can do anything." So I sent it to him.

He called me back several days later and said, "I've got it finished, and I'm fixing to sing it into my little song recorder and send it to you." It was just him, no music, but I heard it and thought it was just gorgeous. Matthew Holt recorded the piano demo; Katy Peach and Joseph sang the parts.

When Jonathan Wilburn was looking for songs for the first Wilburn & Wilburn project with Daywind, he wasn't sure exactly which direction they were going, though he had a pretty good idea. I said, "I'm just going to send you everything. I'm not even going to think about the style. I'm just going to flood you." He literally wanted to hear everything I had. Jonathan and Jordan fell for this one right away.

I was expecting a huge orchestral treatment on the song. But Ben Isaacs was producing, and he told Jordan, "I'm gonna be very stripped out with the instrumentation on it, but when the people hear the harmony background vocals, they're going to think they're hearing musical instruments. They'll have the sensation or the feeling of a big orchestra, but it's going to be voices instead."

When you listen to it from that perspective, you'll realize what he means. He said, "You'll get the full effects you want, but it won't be the big timpani, the big strings and all that." It really is a power ballad, but a power ballad like Ben Isaacs would produce it and Jordan Wilburn would sing it. It just worked.

This song proved to me the chops that Joseph Habedank had, that he could go from "Footprints on the Water" to that. And he's just as strong on lyrics!

The Father and the Son
The Freemans

My brother preached one morning on Abraham and Isaac. It's one of those stories that's been told a lot. I've even written about it before myself, with "God Has Provided a Lamb."

My brother had been talking about Abraham and Isaac were walking up that hill. He used the expression, "with wood on his back." Well, that hit me like an ice pitcher. I reached for the bulletin and jotted it down.

I couldn't wait to contrast the two young men who carried wood on their back up a hill. That afternoon, after I got my last lunch bite down, I picked up the tablet and pencil, and it didn't take all that long.

A major quartet put the song on hold, but my publisher didn't realize that and sent it to The Freemans. When he realized the mistake, he called Darrell and said, "Oh, Darrell, I've made a terrible mistake. That was on hold."

Darrell said that they were already singing the song live. "It's going to be our first single, the centerpiece of our project. We can't not cut it." He wasn't angry; he just really wanted the song! He asked if the publisher could go to the quartet and ask if they would release the song. This is why I will never do my own publishing because I don't want to be the one to call and have that kind of conversation! The quartet was gracious enough to release it.

Ultimately, the right people got it because the Freemans were just meant to sing that song! They even loved the demo so much they got Terry Franklin to come and sing backup vocals on their studio version!

The Maranatha Church Revival
Dove Brothers Quartet

I love to write preacher songs! I liked the idea that it was an elderly preacher who came and pulled a church out of the mullygrubs and got them back on the road to revival. I think it takes an old-time Bible, and, lots of times, an old-time preacher. Even if he's young, I think it needs to be an old-time preacher. Anyone who knows me knows that!

McCray Dove really liked the song, and I liked the cut they did on it.

The Right Side of the Dirt
Legacy Five

As small as my hometown of Blytheville was, it was a hotbed for all kinds of musicians and singers. We had a great barbershop quartet in town, I played piano for beauty pageant contestants, and there was a family of brothers who were fabulous musicians. I knew three of them from school; a fourth brother was a little ol' bitty kid at the time. The second brother, Phil Smith, is one of the best horn players I have ever heard in my life. By high school, he was already fabulous on sax and clarinet. We've always been like brother and sister, and I love him dearly.

Somewhere around 2005, I was recovering from a heart attack at the same time he was recuperating from a hip replacement. I emailed him one day and said, "Well, hon, how's it going? How's everything goin' out there? Are you doin' good?"

He wrote back and used an expression which I had never heard. He said, "Well, I'm still on the right side of the dirt, so I must be doing all right."

I thought, "Oh, my, my, *my*! The right side of the dirt! So how great is that? I know there's a Gospel song in there somewhere."

It came out just funky and fun. When Legacy Five recorded it, the song became Roger's testimony. Cancer had run him through the mill, and every night, he would give an update on his condition.

I was there the night Legacy Five recorded this song live for their *Live in Music City* album. Roger gave the testimony of how he was doing. Every now and then, he would say something really crazy, and add, "Y'all are just going to have to overlook me, I'm on medication. Just act like I didn't say it." He timed things perfectly; at the end, he said, "Well, I guess I could be better, but at the end of it all, I must be doing okay because I'm still on the right side of the dirt." And they kicked it off!

I loved the cut, I loved the way they did it! And I'm telling you, I never heard Glenn Dustin go that low before or since! He nailed that note. When he hit it, everybody in the crowd just went nuts.

That was the last record Roger made with them. In the following months, it became Roger's song, of how to tell how he was doing, and lead into something upbeat, as sad as things were. "I'm still alive, I'm still here, I can still look at my wife and kids."

They did it as long as they had Roger; they haven't done it since. God really used it as a testimony for Roger. It meant everything in the world for me; it's just something God did to show one more facet of the bond that was between us.

The Rock's Between the Hard Place and You
Kingdom Heirs
See Chapter 16.

The Son Came Down
Inspirations

When I wrote it, I got to thinking about the times that the Lord came down. He came down to come to the manger. He came out of the tomb. He's coming down again. I also liked the play on words with the sun coming up and going down.

It turned out to be one that was almost hymnlike. The demo was really stripped down, just piano and Terry Franklin's vocals. There wasn't anything flamboyant about it.

After all my years of writing quartet music, it was the first cut I ever had on an Inspirations record. I wasn't really acquainted with them over the years; I don't think they even knew who I was.

But when I talked to Martin Cook about it, he was just so effusive about what he thought was important about it. He was relating it politically to where our country has gone, and when he would talk about it on stage, he would use the line of the song that says, "Nothing on earth can take Him from us." He would enlarge on how the Devil and everybody who believes like he does are doing all they can to remove Jesus from everything in this country.

His eyes were just shining when he was talking to me. He said, "They can't take my Jesus, they can't take my Jesus."

I thought, "No, darlin', they can't."

I loved the way they did it. I particularly loved it when they would cut away from any kind of music and do a verse a cappella because they really do that so well. Archie Watkins had left the group, but Dallas Rogers had some of Archie's style and he sounded great with them.

I was just honored that they cut it. I love what everybody else loves about the Inspirations—they're doing it right and keeping it real. The image, the suits, the haircuts, the way they behave and present themselves, none of that has changed since 1964. I love that, and their fans have stuck with them because of that. I really didn't want to close out my career and say I never had an Inspirations cut.

There is a Haven
Cathedral Quartet
See Chapter 13.

313

They Went to Pray
The Kingsmen

We were talking about the Mount of Transfiguration in one of my own Sunday School classes. We talked about how there wasn't going to be any trouble getting Moses and Elijah there. Elijah went to Heaven without dying; Moses had already been resurrected, and God got his body away from the devil. So wasn't any stretch for them to come back. I love that whole encounter, and I love the way the Lord gave Peter, James, and John a sneak preview of His glorified state.

The song started coming to me while I was in front of my class. In my head, clear as a CD, I heard, "They went to pray on the mountain," and I thought, "Oh, my! I'm not supposed to be getting a bluesy quartet song out of the teaching! I can't just stop and write this down!"

But my class knows me really well, so I said, "Y'all excuse me just a minute." I took my pencil, and I wrote it at the top of my writing tablet that I had my notes on!

They said, "We know what you're doing! We always know!"

I said, "Well, I can't help it, I can't lose this little part!" As soon as I got home from church, I developed it out.

I love the Kingsmen cut; Harold Reed was just wearing it out!

This Old Place
Ernie Haase & Signature Sound
See Chapter 17.

True to the Call
Kingdom Heirs
See Chapter 16.

Turn Your Back
Cathedral Quartet, Gold City, Triumphant Quartet
See Chapter 8.

We Shall See Jesus
Cathedral Quartet, Ernie Haase & Signature Sound, Legacy Five,
Singing Americans
See Chapter 9.

We Will Stand Our Ground
Kingdom Heirs
See Chapter 16.

What Salvation's Done for Me
Booth Brothers
Also see Chapter 20.

When Rusty Golden and I wrote this song, we had not ever met face to face. He came into my life through a mutual friend, a classmate I had known since the seventh grade. This classmate had a close friend in Alabama, Leon Bruton, who happens to be married to Rusty's mother, Frogene Golden-Bruton. My friend put us in touch, and Frogene and I became email buddies.

In late 2006, when Rusty decided he wanted to come back to Gospel Music, he called his mom and said, "You know, I really don't know anybody in the business anymore, I don't know the trade papers, I don't know what's going on."

She said, "Well, I got a friend who can help you. She writes Gospel Music." Rusty got this image of a little lady with gray hair, who probably wrote hymns or something. I guess he thought if I was close enough to Frogene's age, we must not have anything in common. I should mention here that Frogene is a gorgeous lady who looks *way* too young to have a son Rusty's age!

But anyway, I don't think he was thinking about writing so much, but he did email me. He never met a stranger, so we kind of struck up a friendship. I told him about the Singing News, the websites I followed, and who the big artists were.

We were just writing back and forth. One day, he said, "I'm probably being forward to ask this because I don't even know if you do any co-writing." (Of course, at that point, I had not done a lot.) But, he said, "Would you trust me to work on one with you some time?"

I thought, "Well, he's got William Lee Golden genes—he's probably got the goods! I'll give him a try." So I gave him a lyric that came out as a little quartet song about kicking up gold dust in Heaven. It's never been cut, but he did put a good tune to it. His work tape is the only demo we ever had. I still think we could get it cut if we had the full-out demo.

Not long after that, I began to put the lyrics down on "What Salvation's Done for Me." In my mind, I was hearing the beginnings of a bluesy quartet groove. But something stopped me, and I said, "No, I think I'm going to see what Rusty can do with one like this, because too many of mine come out that way, and I might need a fresh set of ears. Who knows. Let's just see what happens." So I sent him that lyric.

Bear in mind, we had just gotten acquainted. Not long after, he called me, and said, "Well, I finished it, but you're not going to like it."

I said, "Why?"

He said, "It's not quartet a bit."

I said, "Well, I don't just do quartet. Play it and sing it for me." He started playing and singing it for me, and I got a chill. He has a bit of his dad's voice, but it's not a traditional lead-singer voice. But he sings the song with such passion. The Booths did it almost like a lounge tune, with a harmonica, and it works, but Rusty's is more of a power ballad.

There was a second or two I couldn't even speak because I was so moved by it. I said, "Rusty, that's just stunning, what you did with it was just stunning."

He said, "Well, I wasn't going to tell you this till I found out how you felt about it, and you couldn't possibly have known, but you wrote my testimony. I'm that guy."

He had been saved just a few years before that. Jerry Salley, who knew him before and after, told me, "Rusty is a changed person, he got a dose of salvation!"

Rusty told me that he came in late one night. He was tired of living the life of a rock-and-roller. He saw a televangelist preach, and he got right with God that night.

If you haven't had a hard life, you're happy to be saved, but how much more does salvation mean if it brings you a mighty long way? So he identified with every line of that song.

This was when I knew that Rusty and I were going to have a special bond as writers. It was totally unexpected. Even though I'm fourteen years older than he is, we have so much in common. We were both strongly influenced by Godly grandmothers who wrote poetry. Mine raised me, and his did a lot of his raising. We're both children of divorce. I'm widowed and he's never been married, so, of course, we're single and have no children. Our family is our extended family, and we live alone. So we had a lot of common ground.

He could take a lyric that I wrote, completely wed it to a melody, and it would wind up sounding like one person had sat down and written it all. It's just an amazing thing. I saw that happen when we wrote in person, especially when we wrote "God Did it All." When we hit strong, we hit real strong.

In no time after we finished it, he got an invitation from Dean and Mary Brown to be on their live TV show on TBN. So he played and sang our song live. Of course, I was sitting at home watching it. It just so happened that Ronnie Booth was also listening and watching that night and heard the song. He called Rusty, and said, "I just heard the song you did on TBN. I want to record that song. Could you hold it for the next record? I guarantee you we're going to do it." So we did.

Then, pardon the pun, the golden day came when we got word that they were going to send it to radio. The Booths are hotter than a cast-iron skillet on a stove. Not only did it win a Fan Award for Song of the Year, it also won a BMI award for most-played song. It was a huge thing.

I wrote Rusty's testimony and didn't know it!

What We Needed
Kingdom Heirs
See Chapter 16.

When He Washed My Sins Away
Greater Vision, Heaven Bound

I used to write songs short enough to hold out for a nice piano riff in the middle. I did that with this song. When I sent it to Gerald Wolfe, he said, "We absolutely love it, and we want to record it, but we want you to write a second verse to it."

So, of course, what does Dianne say? She says, "Just give me a few minutes."

I thought, "Lord, please don't let me find that I've already said all I wanted to say." I didn't want to add redundant stuff!

Because it was a quartet record, they were doing more of the kinds of songs they did when they started the group. I loved what they did with it!

When Heaven's Gates Swing Open Wide
Kingdom Heirs

Here's what Steve French says about this song: "If you look in the dictionary for the definition of a Southern Gospel timeless song that covers the decades, that should be it."

It has that older, sweet Stamps-Baxter sound, in the same vein as my favorite slow convention song, "Wait Till You See Me in My New Home." The word I keep coming back to for a song like this is "sweet." It's the kind you could play for the older folks in the nursing home; they put their heads back and close their eyes, and think of days gone by.

It came together quickly. I love the instrumentation; it did not overpower the vocal any, and that was great because Jerry Martin sings it like an angel.

When Jesus Comes
Mark Trammell Quartet

When I finished the song, Rick Shelton and I agreed that if it wasn't a Mark Trammell Quartet song, we had never heard one!

It's not a fancy song; it's just a solid Gospel song that would have also worked for someone besides a quartet. I love songs about the Second Coming; I think we're so close, and the older I get, the more I long for Him because of the worse it gets down here.

When Mercy Came Down
Mark Trammell Trio

One year, I was at Quartet Convention. Either I went by myself that year, or Gail had gone off somewhere. I was sitting at one of the big round tables at the food court in the lobby, waiting for a showcase to start.

That song began to come to me of out of nowhere. Sometimes they just come into my head—the whole thing, tune and words. That was one of those times. I don't know that I even had a tablet to write on; I think I had one of those little pads they keep by a telephone in the hotel room.

When I started writing, some of the people around knew who I was. A couple of them said, "I bet we know what you're doing!"

"Well, you probably do! If you ever hear of one called 'When Mercy Came Down,' you'll know you were sitting there when it got started."

When I finished it, I knew it was the kind of doctrinal song that Mark Trammell would love to do, and he took it quickly. It's one of my favorites; I love what it says.

When the Story of My Life Is Told
Kingdom Heirs

This is the one and only time my darlin' little grandson Scotty Inman ever wrote with me in my own house. Triumphant was going to be singing in concert that night at my church. Their bus was parked on the street outside my house. The deal was, the rest of the boys would stay on the bus during the morning. Scotty and I would write. Then they would come in, and I was going to feed them dinner. All afternoon, we were going to sit in my computer room, and they were going to listen to songs. So Scotty and I knew we just had a half a day.

He had the idea of "When the Story of My Life is Told" and approximately what he wanted to say. I had an idea for a tune, so we got it done by noon. I have my equipment set up to make demos, so I played, and he sang the words.

When we got through, he said, "Boy, that was rangy; it was hard for me to reach those high notes!"

And I said, "Welcome to my life! I'm the one always trying to sing those quartet songs and having to squeal at the end! I put a lot of range in 'em on purpose, so you quartet boys can swap leads, because it makes the song interesting."

He said, "Well, I never knew what a struggle you had before today!"

It sure didn't sound like he was struggling!

Triumphant passed on it, but the Kingdom Heirs did it. When it came time to send it to the radio, a totally different kind of song had just been to the radio. They picked it because they wanted to go back to a straight-up quartet song.

When You Look at Me
Kingdom Heirs
See Chapter 16.

Where Jesus Prayed
The Kingsmen

This was during the great period when Tim Surrett was picking songs for the Kingsmen. It predated the movie *The Passion of the Christ*, but it depicted Jesus' suffering vividly enough that people asked if I wrote it after seeing that movie.

Any time Tim Surrett had the lead, I was just so happy because his voice was one of my all-time favorite Gospel Music voices ever. I know he can sing bluegrass and make the angels weep. But he can sing *anything* and make me weep. He just has that gorgeous voice. I was just delighted with the cut.

I have always thought it sounded like something Vince Gill would do if he was going to do a Gospel song. It was made for Vince Gill, but Vince Gill don't need no Dianne songs! He's got Vince songs! But Vince, if you're out there, hon, it's not too late!

Where's John
Kingdom Heirs
See Chapter 16.

Whisper a Prayer
The Kingsmen

This was my first Kingsmen cut. They cut it in 2001, on *I Will*, when Jerry Martin was with them, and Bryan Hutson was singing with them for the first time.

Bryan really sounded like Elvis on this song, and he wasn't even trying! He sang the lead, and then when it went up into the treetops, Jerry took it out on a really high ending. It had some great brass!

It was very bluesy and quartety, like "Steppin' on the Stars" or "Goin' Home Day." I've never been disappointed by a Kingsmen cut, and this is one of my favorite cuts ever. I've just loved all the cuts I've had done with them.

Within the Reach of a Prayer
Collingsworth Family

When Kyla Rowland and I write together, sometimes one of us will write the words, and the other one the tune, but I think we both contributed equally on this one. Joseph Habedank and Katy Peach sang vocals on the demo; a mixed group could certainly hear the beauty in the demo.

Mr. Personality himself, Phil Collingsworth, asked me for upbeat songs. They had picked all their ballads. I was scrolling through what I had, and I saw that song. I played it and thought, "You know, I'll send him some upbeat songs, but I think this sounds like something they would like."

Phil wrote me back and said, "Well, now you've done it! We're going to have to decide which one of the ballads we were going to do to kick off because we are doing this one!" So they did, and oh, what a marvelous cut it was.

If you get a Collingsworth cut, you don't even have to think about if it's going to be good. They are spectacular, and Wayne Haun is their producer, so you're going to get perfection! They just keep getting better and better with each album, even when you think they can't.

It's obvious to me that they rehearse down to the finest little nuance of the detail of one little tiny place in a note. Other people don't always work as hard to make it that perfect. You would expect that if it's this perfect, that it would be a little bit sterile, but it's not. It's that perfect, and yet the Spirit of God is all over it anyway. That's hard, when you've got it absolutely perfect!

I've never had the idea that Kim kept her children standing around the piano till the poor little things are hungry and tired and ready to quit! It's not like that! I just have this sense that they all love it, and that when they're in rehearsal, they just keep working till they get that perfect chord, that perfect blend.

You can play almost any song with the three basic chords, and it would be okay. But Kim is such a musician that she can find chords that probably only three people in the universe can play, and then she's got a kid to sing every one of those notes!

Phil, Kim, and all the kids are absolute delights to know. Their children have been raised to love the Lord and be respectful. They're just a dear, dear family; what you think they ought to be is exactly what they are. I just love them dearly, and I love everything they've done.

Work of Grace
Paid in Full

I do not like hearing about anyone thinking that they got to help the Lord out on their salvation. All the work has been done! There was plenty of work involved in providing grace to me, but it's been done by Somebody else! So I thought "Work of Grace" was a neat way to put it.

The guys with Paid in Full are just darling; I love them dearly. I sent them several songs, and that's the one they picked. Most of the time they didn't feature Jeff Crews on the tenor because Lance Moore is a strong lead singer. But he stepped out on this one. They got a marvelous cut and sent it to radio; it's the only song they ever sent to radio that featured Jeff. I thought he sang it so sweetly; he has an unusual tenor voice.

As much as anything I've ever written, I have had so many requests from men in church choirs, wanting the sheet music of that song so their church choir can sing it. Of course, there's no printed version of it anywhere, so I've always had to say no. It's one of those that I would give anything if I had just shelled out and done what it took to make it available to people.

I don't do a whole lot of ballads, but somehow a lot of my ballads are especially dear to me, and I love that one. I'm very happy that Paid in Full did it; the right ones got it.

You Gotta Go by Grace
The Hoppers

My brother was preaching on a Wednesday night, and he was describing the contrast between law and grace. He said, "The law says you have to stay out, but grace says come on in."

I thought, "Yes, that's exactly right, you gotta go by grace." I began to develop that thought. Nobody can go into the Holy of Holies, but with grace, we can come right to the throne—holy!

Wouldn't you think that with all that deep subject matter, it would have come out a sweet, strong ballad? Well, it didn't! It came out funky!

Dean Hopper called me and wanted to know if I had anything for them. They were getting ready to cut. I said, "Well, my latest one is my favorite, and I don't have have a demo on it!"

He said, "Well, you know that don't bother us! Never has! Just play it and sing it and send it to us!" So I did, and Kim nailed it right up on the wall, just like a picture.

You Gotta Know
Greater Vision, Ivan Parker

This was back in the Centergy days, when I would play piano for my demos and Terry Franklin would sing the demo. In the demo, I played a driving boogie shuffle.

Ivan Parker's cut was fast, and he sent it to the radio. Gerald Wolfe and Greater Vision gave it a Cathedral-esque type treatment.

I liked Ivan's cut, and I was delighted that he did it because he's one of my favorite people ever, just a great guy. When I see him now, I tease him: "Well, I didn't know when you did that one, I never was going to get another one!"

He said, "Well, you don't send me anything—you send it to all those people in groups with four guys on the stage! So we tease each other about that. And I've loved *everything* of mine that Greater Vision ever did!

You'll Still Be There
Wilburn & Wilburn
See Chapter 20.

About the Authors

Dianne Wilkinson has had around fifty charting singles on the industry-standard Singing News monthly radio charts; seven have reached #1. "We Shall See Jesus" was named Song of the Year by the Southern Gospel Music Association in 1984. Two of her songs have received Dove Awards® nominations for Southern Gospel Song of the Year—"Oh, Come Along" (1996) and "The Old White Flag" (2009). Over a dozen of her songs have been nominated for Song of the Year in the Singing News Fan Awards; two, "Jesus Has Risen" (1995) and "What Salvation's Done For Me" (2009), have won.

Daniel J. Mount launched SouthernGospelBlog.com in 2006 and has built it into one of the most-visted Southern Gospel news websites. He is also the author of *The Faith of America's Presidents*, published by AMG/Living Ink in 2007.